12

THE JERUSALEM-HARVARD LECTURES

*Sponsored by the Hebrew University of Jerusalem
and Harvard University Press*

After the Fact

Two Countries, Four Decades,
One Anthropologist

Clifford Geertz

HARVARD UNIVERSITY PRESS
Cambridge, Massachusetts
1995

This book is printed on acid-free paper, and its binding materials have been
chosen for strength and durability.

Library of Congress Cataloging-in-Publication Data
Geertz, Clifford.
  After the fact : two countries, four decades, one anthropologist /
Clifford Geertz.
      p. cm. — (The Jerusalem-Harvard lectures)
  Includes bibliographical references and index.
  ISBN 0-674-00871-5 (acid-free paper)
  1. Geertz, Clifford. 2. Anthropologists—United States—Biography.
  3. Anthropologists—Asia—Biography. 4. Asia—Social conditions.
  5. Africa—Social conditions. 6. Anthropology—Philosophy. I. Title.
  II. Series.
GN21.G44A3   1995
301′.092—dc20

94-12734
    CIP

For Karen

Contents

AFTER THE FACT

1

Towns

*S*uppose, having entangled yourself every now and again over four decades or so in the goings-on in two provincial towns, one a Southeast Asian bend in the road, one a North African outpost and passage point, you wished to say something about how those goings-on had changed. You could contrast then and now, before and after, describe what life used to be like, what it has since become. You could write a narrative, a story of how one thing led to another, and those to a third: "and then . . . and then." You could invent indexes and describe trends: more individualism, less religiosity, rising welfare, declining morale. You could produce a memoir, look back at the past through the blaze of the present, struggling to re-experience. You could outline stages—Traditional, Modern, Postmodern; Feudalism, Colonialism, Independence— and postulate a goal for it all: the withered state, the iron cage. You could describe the transformation of institutions, structures in motion: the family, the market, the civil service, the school. You could even build a model, conceive a process, propose a theory. You could draw graphs.

The problem is that more has changed, and more disjointly, than one at first imagines. The two towns of course have altered, in many ways superficially, in a few profoundly. But so, and likewise, has the anthropologist. So has the discipline within which the anthropologist works, the intellectual setting within which that discipline exists, and the moral basis on which it rests. So have the countries in which the two towns are enclosed and the international world in which the two countries are enclosed. So has just about everyone's sense of what is available from life. It is Heraclitus cubed and worse. When everything changes, from the small and immediate to the vast and abstract—the object of study, the world immediately around it, the student, the world immediately around him, and the wider world around them both—there seems to be no place to stand so as to locate just what has altered and how.

The Heraclitan image is in fact false, or anyway misleading. Time, this sort of time, part personal, part vocational, part political, part (whatever that might mean) philosophical, does not flow like some vast river catching up all its tributaries and heading toward some final sea or cataract, but as larger and smaller streams, twisting and turning and now and then crossing, running together for a while, separating again. Nor does it move in shorter and longer cycles and durations, superimposed one upon another as a complex wave for an harmonic analyst to factor out. It is not history one is faced with, nor biography, but a confusion of histories, a swarm of biographies. There is order in it all of some sort, but it is the order of a squall or a street market: nothing metrical.

It is necessary, then, to be satisfied with swirls, confluxions, and inconstant connections; clouds collecting, clouds dispersing. There is no general story to be told, no synoptic picture to be had. Or if there is, no one, certainly no one wandering into the middle of them like Fabrice at Waterloo, is in a position to construct them, neither at the time nor later. What we can construct, if we keep notes and survive, are hindsight accounts of the connectedness of things that seem to have happened: pieced-together patternings, after the fact.

To state this mere observation about what actually takes place when someone tries to "make sense" out of something known about from assorted materials encountered while poking about in the accidental dramas of the common world is to bring on a train of worrying questions. What has become of objectivity? What assures us we have things right? Where has all the science gone? It may just be, however, that all understanding (and indeed, if distributive, bottom-up models of the brain are right, consciousness as such) trails life in just this way. Floundering through mere happenings and then concocting accounts of how they hang together is what knowledge and illusion alike consist in. The accounts are concocted out of available notions, cultural equipment ready to hand. But like any equipment it is brought to the task; value added, not extracted. If objectivity, rightness, and science are to be had it is not by pretending they run free of the exertions which make or unmake them.

To form my accounts of change, in my towns, my profession, my world, and myself, calls thus not for plotted narrative, measurement, reminiscence, or structural progression, and certainly not for graphs; though these have their uses (as do models and theorizings) in setting frames and defining issues. It calls for showing how particular events and unique occasions, an encounter here, a development there, can be woven together with a variety of facts and a battery of interpretations to produce a sense of how things go, have been going, and are likely to go. Myth, it has been said, I think by Northrop Frye, describes not what happened but what happens. Science, social science anyway, is much the same, save that its descriptions make claim to solider grounding and sounder thought, and aspire, sometimes, to a certain dispassion.

☙

I first went to the Southeast Asian town, Pare, Indonesia, a district seat in the great Brantas river plain of east central Java, in 1952. It was less than two years since the Kingdom of the Netherlands had transferred sovereignty, after five years of scattered and intermittent fighting, to the Republic of Indonesia. I was part of a team of graduate students sent out from Harvard to open up that part of the now unowned world for American social science. There were ten of us, including my then wife, and we arrived in Jakarta by ship three weeks from Rotterdam (Gibraltar, Suez, Colombo, Singapore, names with a romance they now have largely lost) a day after the first attempted coup in the new state's history. There were tanks in the streets, and the political living rooms of the capital were alive with rumors, hopes, dashed hopes, and imaginings of new conspiracies.

I first went to the North African town, Sefrou, Morocco, a district seat at the foot of the Middle Atlas Mountains thirty kilometers due south of Fez, in 1963, with the notion of perhaps setting up there a rather different sort of collective study. (I was, by then, an assistant professor at the University of Chicago, positioning graduate students much as I had myself been positioned.) It was about six years after the end of the French Protectorate, and Muhammad V, the charismatic hero-king who had returned from French-imposed exile in Madagascar to capture the nationalist movement and lead his people to independence, had suddenly died after a nasal operation, supposed to be minor. His son, Hassan II, thirty-two years old, a hard-set military figure and reputedly something of a sports-car playboy, a Moroccan Prince Hal, had just been precipitated onto the throne. Amid a passionate outburst of mass grief, frightening sometimes in its sheer abandon, the political cafés of Rabat—where, having flown in, more or less on impulse, from a sort of anthropology summit conference in Britain, I then was living—were humming with suspicions about the old king's death, doubts about the new one's staying power, and speculations about who would be the first to test it.

Entry of this sort into an entr'acte where all the really critical things seem just to have happened yesterday and just about to happen tomorrow, induces an uncomfortable sense of having come too late and arrived too early, a sense which in my case never afterward left me. In Pare or in Sefrou, in 1952, 1958, 1963, 1964, 1966, 1969, 1971, 1972, 1976, or 1986, it always seemed not the right time, but a pause between right times, between a turbulence somehow got through and another one obscurely looming. Change, apparently, is not a parade that can be watched as it passes.

Pare in the early fifties was a shabby, alternately hot and dusty and hot and muddy crossroads town of perhaps twenty thousand (a couple thousand of them Chinese), and the regional hub, depending on how and for what purposes you defined its hinterland, for anywhere between a hundred thousand and a quarter million villagers. A few years away from its first, and, as it turned out, last, experience with genuinely open parliamentary elections, it, with the countryside around it, was caught up in a rising clamor of political bitterness. Four major parties, each determined, or so it seemed, to capture absolute power and do away, legally if possible, physically if necessary, with the others, dominated public life, and made of it, as it also turned out, a prelude to killing fields. Two of these parties were religious, that is, Islamist, one purportedly progressive and reformist, one purportedly traditional and revivalist, though the differences between them were more cultural than anything else. The other two were at least ostensibly secular, though much encrusted with local belief and deeply hostile to all forms of rigorist Islam: a so-called Nationalist Party, claiming fidelity to the glowing, if rather haphazard, ideas of Indonesia's founding spirit, President Sukarno, and the Communist Party, the largest then outside the Sino-Soviet bloc.

The elections were held in 1955, precisely a year after I left. By the time I got back in 1971 (having been to Morocco—and to Bali—in the meantime), the killing fields had come and gone, the national regime had changed from civilian to military, and what politics existed was dominated by a semi-official umbrella party promoting a semi-official civil religion. Pare was still physically about what it had been. With a net outflow of population nearly matching natural increase, it was not even much larger. The same people, the same groups (though there were no Communists, and fewer Sukarnoists), the same bureaus, were still in charge, and most of them operated with the same, formal and status-ridden, ideas of right and propriety. Daily life, except for the fact that the ideologues were quiet or silenced, was not much different, nor, the Green Revolution only beginning to take hold, was the economy. What was different, or anyway seemed different to me, was mood, humor, the color of experience. It was a chastened place.

In the 1955 elections the Communists won about three-quarters of the town vote, the revivalist Muslims about three-quarters of the village vote. The Sukarnoists and the reformist Muslims divided most of the rest, though as they were rooted among the more influential elements in both town and countryside, the result was less lopsided in power terms than the sheer numbers might suggest. But it was lopsided enough, and it got rapidly more so as the decade wore on. A nasty surprise to both the winners and the losers, who suddenly realized what high stakes they were playing for and how near the showdown was, the election results led to an explosion of to-the-knife conceptions of political combat. An "it's us or them" frenzy descended upon the town and the region around it, not to be dispersed until the 1965 bloodbath finally determined who was the us, who the them.

This furious mixture of fear and bravado was pervasive in Pare as early as 1958, when I visited it for a week during the time I was working in Bali. (It had not yet set in on that supposedly dreaming island, though it eventually did so with a vengeance and, if anything, an even bloodier outcome.) In the country at large, the balance among the major parties in the 1955 election was reasonably even. The Sukarnoists and the reformist Muslims got a shade more than a fifth of the vote each, the revivalist Muslims and the Communists a shade less. In its polarized state between popular radicalism and popular revivalism, romantic democracy right and left, as well as in the relentlessness of its passions, Pare was thus atypical. But, a moral for enthusiasts of statistical "representativeness" as the only basis for generalization, and for those who think large-scale conclusions can come only from large-scale investigations, it turned out, over the course of the decade, to have been marvelously predictive of things to come: the leading edge of national disaster.

After the elections, and most especially after 1959, when Sukarno, beset, as he put it in that expansive way of his, like Dante in the *Divina Commedia* by the devils of liberalism, individualism, adventurism, factionalism, rebellion, and the multi-party system, suspended constitutional democracy, the politics of terror took hold in Pare with astonishing speed. Squatters flooded onto former Dutch plantation lands and forcibly resisted government efforts to remove them, leading to capsized tractors, swishing sickles, and panic shootings. Muslim youths organized paramilitary training centers, which were then attacked by Communist youths. Share-cropping peasants, enraged by evasions of land reform laws, pronounced the fields they were working their own and challenged the legal owners to do something about it. The reformist Muslim party was banned, driving the religious rightward; Sukarno backed away from the Nationalists, driving the secularists leftward. Mass rallies became daily affairs, increasingly large, increasingly aggressive. Parades of shouting militants marched on government offices. Civil servants cowered in their houses. Religious schools were attacked. Left-wing newspaper distributors had their offices trashed. "Outside agitators" arrived from all directions calling for the elimination of imperialist satans or soulless kaffirs. Weapons got distributed. Lists got drawn up. Letters got sent.

Panic and intransigence grew, thus, in tandem, mutually reinforcing one another and deepening the conviction that the losers were really going to lose and the winners really to win. When the massacres finally arrived, they seemed, as do most popular convulsions—takings of Winter Palaces, stormings of Bastilles—a postscript to a story long in the writing. If, as the local leader of the Nationalist Party, you know not only that the Left has marked you for a festive execution but that it plans to use your grand and rambling house as its Kremlin afterward, or, if, as the head of a Communist peasant union, you have seen yourself, horned, tailed, and hanging from a crescent, stenciled onto various walls around town, the actual eruption of violence comes more as a completion, a rounding off, than as a breaking into something new. The oft-remarked end-game quality of the massacres, the readiness and near-ritual calm, some called it resignation, others dissociation, with which the victimized delivered themselves up to those who victimized them, had less to do with cultural attitudes or the power of the army, both of which were more agent than impetus, than with the fact that ten years of ideological polarization had convinced virtually everyone that the only thing remaining to be seen was which way, in the event, the balance would tip.

It tipped, of course, in the rightward direction. The failure of the palace guard coup in Jakarta at the end of September 1965, a confused and brutal affair still ill-understood, led to a series of small-scale iterations of it as its example spread, place by place, across Java and on to Bali, west to east. In each place there was the initial uncertainty, lasting a day or two at most, as to which way things would go. Then there was the realization on all sides, usually in the space of hours, as to which way, always the same way, things would go. Then there were the killings, halted after a while by the army. In each locality the whole convulsion took hardly more than two or three weeks (in my Balinese village it took one night, during which thirty families were burned alive in their houses), was repressed or subsided, and then moved on to be repeated eastward, summing, after about five months, to perhaps a quarter million, perhaps three quarters of a million deaths.

The killing got to Pare in early November, set off there when a countryside religious teacher, whose father, a reformist leader, I had worked with in 1952, made a reconnaissance into an adjoining village, where my colleague Robert Jay had worked, to check out rumors that peasant union militants there were about to attack, and was stabbed to death. His compatriots retaliated the following night by setting fire to a large number of houses in the offending village, after which right-to-left assaults exploded, incident by incident, across the whole area. Rather than retail cases, a newspaper or TV roundup of the day's atrocities, let me instead quote an account of "what it was like then" given to me by that Nationalist Party leader—by 1971 retired, disheartened, and done (or almost) with patrician maneuvering—whom I mentioned earlier as marked for death and expropriation. (I omit my prompt questions, which were merely that: the psychiatrist's ineffable "Ah, yes?" and "Why do you say that?")

> Nineteen sixty-five was as bad here as anywhere in the country. Most of the killings were by Muslim youth groups. Except for Plosok Klaten [an outlying village near the squatter areas], where there was a brief battle between the Communists and the Muslims, which the Muslims, helped by the army, soon won, the Communists all just

surrendered, confessed openly to plotting, and were killed, unresisting, next to open graves which the Muslims had waiting for them. (The Communists had graves ready for the Muslims too, in case things went their way.)

This was a weird reaction, even to me, a Javanese who has lived around here all his life. Apparently, the Communists reasoned: "If I'm dead, that's an end of it. It's 'settled,' 'complete,' 'cleaned up,' 'finished' [*bèrès*]. But if I'm arrested, I'll suffer. There will be no food. I will be in prison." So they just accepted "The End" [*puputan*].

Everyone here was terrified. A Communist leader's head was hung up in the doorway of his headquarters. Another's was hung on the footbridge in front of his house with a cigarette stuck between his teeth. There were legs and arms and torsos every morning in the irrigation canals. Penises were nailed to telephone poles. Most of the killing was by throat cutting and stabbing with bamboo spears.

The whole population of a village would be herded onto the public square in front of the District Office by the army. They were then told to point out who was an activist and who was not. The activists were then delivered back to the people to take home and execute, or, more often, handed over to people of neighboring villages in exchange for their victims. That made it easier, because you weren't killing your next door neighbor, but someone else's who was killing yours.

At one point, there was a rumor that the town was going to be attacked by leftists from Sekoto [the village in which the religious teacher had been killed]. Tanks came from Kediri [the regional capital] and there was firing all night and in the morning almost everyone from Sekoto had been rounded up. They were asked if they had intended to attack the town and kill the local officials. They answered yes and gave details. Five of the leaders were executed in the public square by the army, the others were let go to be dealt with by their neighbors, who took them back to the village and killed them.

All this lasted only about a month, but it was a terrible month. There was no one in the streets at all. Women were killed as well as men, but, though a few stores were looted, no Chinese were harmed. They were not involved: it was a matter between Javanese. Most of the important Communist leaders were not Pare people by that time, because the party moved their cadres around every few months, like the civil service. One of the most prominent local leaders—a man named Guntur—hanged himself, but others escaped to the larger cities where they hoped they would be less noticeable. Local doctors would not treat Communist wounds, because they were threatened with death if they did so. My younger brother saw three people executed at the District Office, there were lots of people watching, and he couldn't sleep for a week.

In the beginning, things could have gone either way. Each side was trying to kill the other side first, and when the Communists saw that the Muslims had the upper hand, they just gave up. There was no resistance from the Left at all, once the killings began. The army, which was upset by the murders of the general staff in Jakarta at the time of the coup, just let the Muslim youth have their head, at least for a while, after which they called a halt and began just arresting people and carting them off to Buru [a prison island in eastern Indonesia] or somewhere.

There is still a good deal of bad feeling around on the part of friends and relatives of the victims. But anti-Communism is now so strong here they don't dare say anything; they just conceal it, like good Javanese. I myself am as anti-Communist as I always was. But the real hatred, the murdering and the being murdered, was a matter between Muslim militants and Communist ones. Sukarno people, like me, were, in the end, really just bystanders. Like, in the end, Sukarno himself.

If in 1971, six years after the event, all this was but a bad memory, by 1986, twenty-one years after, it hardly seemed a memory at all, but a broken piece of history, evoked, on occasion, as an example of what politics brings. Those branded as having been Communists or supporters of them (twelve percent of the electorate, five percent in the town) could not vote or hold a government job, but were not otherwise much bothered. Faded maps showing the location of Communist households, including the one I had lived in in 1953–1954, still hung, like folk ornaments, on village office walls. Aging Muslim militants occasionally reflected, especially when confronted by an outsider who had known them when both were young, on how close they had come to a messy end. But, in general, the town was like a pond across which a terrible storm had once swept, a long time ago, in another climate.

For someone who had known it before the storm, the place seemed to have exchanged the gathered-up energies of politics for the scattered-out ones of trade. The conjunction of the Green Revolution, which began to be effective in this part of Java only toward the end of the seventies when problems of implementation got finally worked out, and the settling in of military rule, which found an operational style to suit its conception of itself as an engine of progress at about the same time, led to a commercialization of town life at least as pervasive, and nearly as obsessive, as its politicization once had been. Buying and selling—diverse, intricate, virtually continuous buying and selling, reaching into all levels and corners of society and operating on all sorts of scale and degrees of extension—replaced getting ready for doomsday as the dominant preoccupation of just about everyone. A peasant agriculture drawn bodily into the market by an increased need for capital inputs, an officially homogenized political life, and a lingering sense that both were precarious had brought on the tone and look of an enormous, bustling, rather driven emporium.

The temptation to take this state of affairs as a terminus point, the completion of a phase, a process, a development, now to be but secured and extended, is great and must be resisted. When after a great convulsion a mere busyness occurs, the sense that things are at last on track arises of itself, especially in a before-and-after witness like me, if not among those who have passed through it all and have some reason to imagine otherwise. The stories one tells naturally take on a beginning, middle, and end, a form coincident less with the inner direction of things than with one's parenthetic experience of them. To remove the parenthesis is to misrepresent at once how you got what you think might be knowledge and why you think it might be.

Sefrou in the early sixties, by then perhaps a thousand years old, still had a sharpness of definition extraordinary even for Morocco, where everything seems outlined in calcium light. When you approached the town from Fez, then thirty kilometers away, today only twenty, coming up over a small rise from the north, you found yourself confronted with the same scene that had astonished a whole series of earlier experience seekers—Leo Africanus in the sixteenth century, Père Foucauld in the nineteenth, Edith Wharton during the First World War—who stumbled upon what one of them (Foucauld) called "l'Oasis enchanteresse," another (Wharton) "a stout little walled town with angle-towers defiantly thrust toward the Atlas." The town, the oasis, the mountains, each enclosed within the next, chalk white, olive green, stone brown, each marked off from the next by a line so sharp as to seem drawn with a pen, gave a sense of deliberate arrangement. Site and settlement looked equally designed.

The initial effect of going on then to descend into the body of the town was, for a foreigner anyway, the total, instantaneous, and, so it seemed for an uncomfortable period, permanent dissolution of this sense of clarity, poise, and composition. Neither the population, in 1961 perhaps twenty thousand, nor the layout of the place was in any way simple or homogeneous. Berbers, Arabs, Jews, merchants, notables, tribesmen, artisans, even still a few French *colons,* teachers, and administrators, coursed through narrow alleys, broad thoroughfares, sprawling bazaars. Part of the city was a maze, part was a grid, part was a coil of winding suburban roads. There were mosques, parks, crenelated walls, caravanserais, moorish baths, lime kilns, waterfalls, tiled fountains, grilled windows, tennis courts, interior gardens, motion picture theaters, castle-houses, schools, sheep pens, black tents, and sidewalk cafes; and everywhere the sound of urgent talk, mostly male. A French-built fort out of *Beau Geste* looked down on all this from one knoll, a white-domed Muslim shrine out of *En Tribu* looked down on it from another. By the towering main gate there were a cemetery, a swimming pool, a bus terminal, an oil press, an outdoor mimbar, a porter's station, an experimental garden, a bowling green, an old prison, and a tea house. A half mile away there was a cave where Jews lit candles to mythic rabbis.

As so often happens, such first impressions, because they are first, and perhaps as well because they are impressions rather than worked-up theories or pinned-down facts, set a frame of perception and understanding, a Jamesian hum of buzz and implication, that could not afterward be wholly discarded, only critiqued, developed, filled out, moralized upon, and brought to bear on more exact experiences. The double image, clarity from a distance, jumble up close, not only did not dissolve over the twenty-five years or so I off and on worked in Sefrou and in the district around it (another seventy or eighty thousand people, divided into dozens of "fractions," "tribes," "circles," and "confederations"), it turned into my most general conception of what it was that was driving things: an ascending tension between a classic urban form Ibn Khaldun would have found familiar and a swelling and diversifying urban life tumbling across its incised lines. A place where nothing very spectacular happened, and which remained agrarian, peripheral, and rather traditional, it steadily, carelessly, got instructively out of hand.

In 1963, this process had already begun, but only barely. The old walled city, with its satellite "casbah" standing guard above it and its Jewish "mellah" gated-off in the center of it, still dominated the scene. A few "native quarters," squared corners and straightened streets, had been built under French direction just outside the walls; a small villa area, shade trees and swimming pools, had grown up during the Protectorate; and some glass-front stores had appeared along the highroad. But the place was still your basic, textbook *medīna:* a labyrinth-fortress set round with irrigated olive groves, and divided between deeply urban Arabs, long in place, and deeply urban Jews (still three thousand of them, down from a peak of five or six), quite possibly in place—some of them claimed since the Exodus—even longer.

In 1986, the old city was dwarfed by new quarters spreading out rudely and irregularly in all directions around it. The French and the Jews ("our heads and our pockets," as the Arabs called them with uncertain irony) had departed, but there were three times as many people, most of them country-born Berbers. Perhaps eighty percent of the adult population had lived there less than twenty years, two-thirds less than ten. The settled area had quadrupled. Half of the olive groves had disappeared beneath buildings, and the rest were going. It hardly seemed the same place.

During the first phases of my and my colleagues' work, the internal complexity of the place seemed reasonably well contained within an at least somewhat orderly set of customs, classes, and institutions. It was still possible to divide the population into broad, more or less recognizable groups, and life proceeded, if not exactly to plan, anyway along discernible lines. There was a rooted elite, a handful of "old Sefrou" Arab families who had virtually monopolized social, economic, and religious power since well before the Protectorate. (Perhaps two percent of the population, they controlled perhaps fifty percent of the oasis land, and had extended holdings in the countryside as well.) There was a small set of royal administrators, almost all of them brought in for limited terms from someplace else, carrying out the daily functions of government, which largely consisted of conveying regulations, issuing permits, witnessing contracts, and arresting people. The relatively few countryfolk who had migrated in had settled into the abandoned Jewish quarter. (The Jews themselves had moved outside the walls.) Residential quarters were discrete, trades molecular, bazaars specialized. The overwhelming majority of the population, including the Jews, were native speakers of Arabic, had been born in the city, were occupied in some way or other, usually complicated, with marketplace commerce. There were a half dozen mosques, two or three synagogues, a shariah court, and a Catholic church. For all the commotion, it seemed eminently studyable.

And so it was, for a while. The longstanding alliance of a small, locally entrenched power elite and an even smaller, soldier-backed collection of caids, pashas, sheikhs, and qadis, directly dependent upon central authority, made politics a fairly elementary, whowhom affair. For a short period after the attainment of Independence, which involved a certain amount of guerrilla activity around Sefrou, a surge of party agitation, Muslim and populist on the one side, Marxist and populist on the other, threatened, slightly, this alliance and the command-post style of government it represented; but, particularly after Hassan II consolidated his position, the status quo was quickly restored. In the sixties and through most of the seventies, Sefrou not only looked like a classic medina, Moroccan style, an enchanted oasis defying the Atlas, "a little Fez"; for the most part, it behaved like one.

To the professionalized mind, bent on structure, the city divided all too easily into parts and subparts. There was the residential system: a dozen quarters, each with a name, a head, a gate, a public oven, a public fountain, a public bath, and a public prayer house, and each sectioned into alleyway neighborhoods, also named, headed, and dominated by one or another of the old families. There was the economic system: a trade and craft sector, clustered around the grand mosque at the center of the old city, almost obliterating it from view, or scattered in weekly, farmerish bazaars beyond the walls; and an agricultural sector, small-scale olive tenders and wheat growers, mostly share-croppers, in the oasis. The leading trades, including agriculture, were grouped into "guilds," the "guilds" were headed by "guild chiefs," and the "guild chiefs" were presided over by a sort of commercial judge. There was the religious system: mosques, Quranic schools, Sufi brotherhoods, a clerical class of officiants and legal scholars, the shariah court, a mortmain religious foundation to which most of the commercial property and much of the agricultural belonged, and Jewish counterparts of each of these. There was the kinship system: the usual patrilineal, patrilocal, patriarchal sort of business; intensely marked sexual difference, arranged marriage, bride price, partible inheritance, ready divorce. There was the political system: government offices, a municipal council, various sorts of tribunals, various sorts of associations, various sorts of police. The place was not only made for a monograph; it sorted itself into chapters.

By 1986, with the accelerating rush of changes, this was no longer so. Of course, even the initial image of settled arrangement was something of a schoolbench story, and the earlier phases of our work there mainly consisted in showing, with some determination, that this was the case: that quarters were multiform, that "guilds" were not really guilds, "guild heads" were not really heads, and "market judge" was a title in search of an occupation; that kinship worked rather differently in practice from the way it worked in theory; that women had ways to get across boundaries and around men; that power-mongering did not stay on the rails laid down for it; and that not all the brotherhoods were quite what they seemed. But the point is that it is no longer possible for even the most methodical anthropologist, eyes fixed on shape and coherence, to tell that kind of story now. The parts are pieces, the whole is an assemblage, and the grand categories of comparative ethnography seem blunt and ill-made.

When trying to comprehend how this condition came to be, one reaches instinctively not for the critical event—fateful incident is hard to discern—but for the eloquent statistic. There are lots of candidates: population growth (two hundred percent in twenty-five years); increased "Islamicity" (eighty percent Muslim in 1960, one hundred in 1986); "illiterization" (a quarter of the adults literate in 1960, a tenth in 1986); "breaching of the walls" (ninety percent of the immigration since 1912 in the last two decades); explosion of residential land prices (a thousand percent between 1960 and 1970). But perhaps the single most telling statistic is the change in the ratio of urban to rural population in the Sefrou district (two thousand square kilometers, where Sefrou, ten square kilometers, is the only town of significant size): one to four in 1960, one to one in 1986. The deserted village, overurbanization, the flight from the land, agro-capitalism, the pull of bright lights; whatever you call it or whatever you attribute it to, the mobbing of Sefrou has been massive, relentless, rapid, and, unless something very odd indeed should occur, irreversible.

It has also been, and not merely for the mobbed, disorganizing. The town is divided, and is seen to be divided, between old inhabitants, "Real Sefrouis" as they call themselves, unhappy with the present because it is not the past, and recent immigrants, "Outsiders" as everyone, including themselves, calls them, unhappy with it because it is not the future. The old inhabitants see the town as becoming an enormous, misshapen village, and their world as besieged. The immigrants see it as an entrenched, impermeable network of courthouse privilege, indifferent to their interests and hostile to their very presence. A power struggle, a class war, and perhaps most stubborn of all a culture clash: a citied society trying to hold off, a country multitude trying to break in.

The result of this for an observer (though not only, and not most importantly, for an observer) is design and clarity obscured yet again by instant jumble. The old city, decayed and quiescent, is engulfed in an urban sprawl, the bazaars have become diffuse and unfocused, political life is both less compact and less directed, religion has lost definition and gathered energy, women are going out to work. The sense that one is continually putting together ordered pictures and having them come apart just at the moment one gets them more or less put together; that the tension between an urban tradition a long way from dead (and, indeed, in some ways revitalizing as its heirs regroup to defend it) and an urban life outrunning that tradition's categories is pervasive, chronic, and not obviously resolvable; and that whatever happens one will never see again that chiseled view from the Fez-road rise, nor even those chapter titles of the nineteen sixties, leaves one as much one of the objects of change as its surveyor, analyst, judge, or chronicler. It is no more possible to escape the situational immediacies of ethnographical knowing, the thoughts and occasions one is trying to intrude upon, than it is to escape its temporal bounds, and it is perhaps even more mischievous to pretend to do so.

☙

Such, such are the facts. Or, anyway, so I say. The doubts that arise, whether in me or my audience, have only very partially to do with questions about the empirical basis upon which these accounts, or others like them, rest. The canons of anthropological "proof" being what they are (mimicries of sterner enterprises like mechanics or physiology), that is, indeed, how such doubts are most often phrased and, to the degree that they are, most often quieted. Footnotes help, verbatim texts help even more, detail impresses, numbers normally carry the day. But, in anthropology anyway, they remain somehow ancillary: necessary of course, but insufficient, not quite the point. The problem—rightness, warrant, objectivity, truth—lies elsewhere, rather less accessible to dexterities of method.

Partly it lies in what these grand idealities are taken to mean. (What is "objectivity" supposed to prevent: passion, relativity, intuitionism, prejudice? What does "rightness" recommend: precision, fidelity, suasiveness, authenticity?) But, more critically, it lies in the workings of the discourse they are designed to improve. How comes it, after all, that, beginning with glancing experiences and half-witnessed events, one ends, as one sometimes does, with formed, written, recounted fact? Mainly, it seems, by way of summary figures somehow assembled along the way: worked-up images of how matters connect. Deciding, and it is a decision, to stage Pare as political agon and picturize Sefrou as moral landscape lays out the world my description describes. Whatever reality is, besides existent, our sense of it (polarized difference, choreographed brutality, obsessive busyness; modeled shape, migrant swarming, social blur) comes inevitably out of the way we talk about it.

The question is, where does the way we talk about it come from? Again, the preferred answer is that it comes from what it is that, with our eyes wide open, our interests set aside, and our methods deployed, we find before us. Everything is what it is and not another thing; agons are agons, landscapes are landscapes. Conceptions—beliefs, views, versions, judgments—may be invented, borrowed from others, derived from theories; they may even be come across in dreams or taken out of poems. But it is the way matters stand that authorizes their use. The essential task is to tell it like it is.

Well, I suppose so; I certainly would not want to try to defend the contrary. Whether, however, this way of looking at matters (ideas put together in the head, things subsisting in the world, and the latter cutting the former to size) is of much help in understanding how knowledge is come by in anthropological work is doubtful. Asking whether Pare really is a succession of contestings or Sefrou really is a dissolving shape is a bit like asking whether the sun really is an explosion or the brain really is a computer. The issue is: What do you say in saying that? Where does it get you? There are other figurations—the sun is a furnace, Sefrou is a bear garden; Pare is a dance, the brain is a muscle. What recommends mine?

What recommends them, or disrecommends them if they are ill-constructed, is the further figures that issue from them: their capacity to lead on to extended accounts which, intersecting other accounts of other matters, widen their implications and deepen their hold. We can always count on something else happening, another glancing experience, another half-witnessed event. What we can't count on is that we will have something useful to say about it when it does. We are in no danger of running out of reality; we are in constant danger of running out of signs, or at least of having the old ones die on us. The after-the-fact, *ex post,* life-trailing nature of consciousness generally—occurrence first, formulation later on—appears in anthropology as a continual effort to devise systems of discourse that can keep up, more or less, with what, perhaps, is going on.

Building systems of discourse, structures of representation within which what might be going on can be set out as assertions and arguments, dressed with evidence, is what anthropologists who claim, as most of us still do, to be recounting things that are indeed the case are up to. And up against. It is to such systems, structures, configurations of signs, ways of saying, not to the deliverances of reality, which only seers are privy to, that doubts and objections are properly addressed. My tale of two towns is not designed merely to establish difference; it is designed to put it to interpretive use. Beginning where I was obliged to begin, with local occasions, I want, now that I am removed from their immediate pressure, to develop a way of talking about matters that transcend and engulf such occasions, and fold, in turn, back upon them—to elaborate a language of significative contrast that can, as I said earlier, make some sort of sense of the swirls and confluxions into whose midst I have, over the years, so clumsily stumbled.

For an ethnographer everything is a matter of one thing leading to another, that to a third, and that to one hardly knows what. Beyond Pare and Sefrou, around them, behind them, standing before them, hovering over them, is an enormous array of—what shall I call them? practices? epistemes? social formations? realities?—that connect to them, and that must find a place in any project which seeks to gain from messing around in them something more than odd information. However difficult it may be to begin this sort of discourse, it is even harder to stop it.

One works *ad hoc* and *ad interim,* piecing together thousand-year histories with three-week massacres, international conflicts with municipal ecologies. The economics of rice or olives, the politics of ethnicity or religion, the workings of language or war, must, to some extent, be soldered into the final construction. So must geography, trade, art, and technology. The result, inevitably, is unsatisfactory, lumbering, shaky, and badly formed: a grand contraption. The anthropologist, or at least one who wishes to complicate his contraptions, not close them in upon themselves, is a manic tinkerer adrift with his wits: Richard Wilbur's Tom Swift, putting dirigibles together, in the quiet weather, out in the backyard.

Countries

*T*he world divides into countries. Aside from the poles and the oceans, a few islands in the Pacific, Caribbean, and south Atlantic, the Vatican, the Canal Zone, Gibraltar, for the moment the West Bank and until 1997 Hong Kong, until 1999 Macao, virtually no spot on the globe is not included in a bounded, continuous stretch of space called the Republic of this, the People's Republic of that, the Union, Kingdom, Emirate, Confederation, State, or Principality of something or other. These stretches are disjunct (no spot can belong to two), categorical (a spot either belongs or it does not), and exhaustive (no spot goes un-belonged), and, now that Pakistan and Bangladesh are two, uninterrupted. Whatever the disputes that take place within its trim definings—Northern Ireland and the Western Sahara, Southern Sudan and Eastern Timor, the spastic tribulations of the redivided lands that used to make up the Soviet Union—we have, by now, an absolute map. Absolute not in the sense that it never changes; Rand McNally has to put out a new edition virtually every day, these days. Absolute in the sense that, however it changes, it is made up of "countries," populated by "peoples," and identified as "states," indeed as "nation-states."

It was, of course, not always thus, and for much of the world it has become so only recently. The scattered empires, culture regions, commercial leagues, city states, condominiums, dependencies, protectorates, free ports, unexplored territories, unbordered dynasties, mandates, and semi-sovereign colonies that dot any historical atlas (Transylvania, East India, Turkestan, the Congo, Tangiers) are but yesterday disappeared, and the politic British archaeologist who titled a book on Indus antiquities *Five Thousand Years of Pakistan* was looking not backwards but sideways. One cannot write a history of "Morocco" or "Indonesia" (the first derives, in the sixteenth century, from a city name, the second, in the nineteenth, from a linguistic classification) that goes back much beyond the 1930s, not because the places didn't exist before then, or the names either, or even because they were not independent, but because they were not countries. Morocco was dynasties, tribes, cities, and sects, and later on *colons.* Indonesia was palaces, peasants, harbors, and hierarchies, and later on *indische heren.* They did not sum to colored polygons.

In both countries, as they now at length more or less are, the seeming finality of their becoming such blots out much of a sense, even among those who know some history, that they are only recently real. For the people who live there, now called citizens, and those who don't, but come as tourists, diplomats, businessmen, journalists, resident aliens, spies, or anthropologists, the suffusive mists of cartographic identity—even the sheep seem Moroccan, even the volcanoes seem Indonesian—make it difficult to remember that places are accidents and their names ideas. The citizenship feels new, at least to the citizens, but the identity does not: we have not always had a state, or have had too many; but we have, if not forever, at least since paddy and Barabudur, Islam and the Arab invasions, always been us.

This disposition, not unqualified but nearly such, to view culture, geography, politics, and self in the blocked-out spaces of the absolute map, as a matter of countries, leads to a conception of the past as prologue and the future as dénouement—history with a permanent subject. This is not precisely whiggism, though the arrow of time certainly points upward and the sense of progress out of a dark past to a less dark present is very strong. Nor is it merely presentism, though the way things are right now dominates perception almost totally. It is rather more what might be called the illusion of quiddity. Within the bloated categories of regime description, Feudalism or Colonialism, Late Capitalism or The World System, Neo-Monarchy or Parliamentary Militarism, there is a resident suchness, deep Moroccanicity, inner Indonesianness, struggling to get out.

Such a conception of things is usually called nationalism. That is certainly not wrong, but, another bloated category, grouping the ungroupable and blurring distinctions internally felt, it is less definite than it seems. Every quiddity has its own form of suchness, and no one who comes to Morocco or Indonesia to find out what goes on there is likely to confuse them with each other or to be satisfied with elevated banalities about common humanity or a universal need for self-expression. Coming into the country, virtually any country, but certainly these, is an experience palpable enough to be felt on the skin, and penetrant enough to be felt beneath it.

The difficulty lies in articulating that experience, making it available to common view. Impressionism, invocations of camels and minarets, rice terraces and shadow puppets, produces a travel poster view of things. Empiricism, magpie amassment of cultural detail, produces an ethnographical telephone book. And thematicism, grand sentiments and large ideas, produces historical opera. Yet Morocco, the Riviera South, is something of a poster, Indonesia, three thousand islands (fourteen thousand, if you count the rocks) and perhaps a couple hundred languages, a bit of a telephone book, and both of them, never quiet for very long, are historical operas; and so such images, as vulgar and reductive as they are (and they are not the worst—zealotic Morocco and dreaming Indonesia are probably that), are where one, perforce, begins when one starts to think about where one is, and, then, after the fact, works to replace them with something a little less summary, a little less external, and a little less charged.

And there is, as well, for anyone who wishes to speak of the two countries in the same breath, the vexing question of similarity and difference. Certainly they are unlike. Indonesia has (as of 1989) about seven times the population, four times the area, four times the Gross Domestic Product, three-fifths the urbanization, twice the growth rate, a bit under half the per capita income, four times the foreign trade, and twice the school enrollment of Morocco. Morocco was colonized by the French and Spanish for about forty years; Indonesia, by the Dutch for about three hundred and fifty. Morocco is hot, dry, and Afro-littoral, wedged between Atlantic storms and Saharan ones; Indonesia, warm, moist, and Malayo-archipelagic, soaked by Asian winds for half the year, dried by Australian ones for the other half. Indonesia has oil, Morocco does not; Morocco has phosphates, Indonesia does not. Wheat, olives, oranges, and wool; rice, sugar, coffee, and rubber. Veils and sarongs, horsemanship and ballet. The kissed ring; the horizontal nod.

But there are striking similarities as well. Both are Islamic; Morocco almost entirely so, Indonesia predominantly. Each has emerged, after the grand jolts to European prestige of the Second World War—Japanese occupation, Vichy collaboration—from a protracted and bitter nationalist revolution; Indonesia's a bit more popular, Morocco's a bit more focused. They have (again, as of 1989) about the same life expectancy, structure of production, rate of population increase, debt service ratio, inflation level, ratio of export earnings to GNP, and per capita calorie supply. Both have been civilized for a millennium, harassed by the West for five centuries, and politically stable, as such things go in what the World Bank (from which these various figures come) carefully calls "lower middle income developing countries," for twenty-five years. Both have inassimilable, or anyway unassimilated, minorities—Jews in the one case, Chinese in the other. Neither is rich, destitute, Marxist, or democratic; nor, as yet, religiously excited.

To say what, exactly, a country is, to characterize it as a social reality with a shape and a force, is, thus, a rather more complicated thing to do than either the plane figure images of the absolute map or the monographic ease with which one talks about Moroccan Agriculture or Indonesian Cooking, The Moroccan Carpet or The Indonesian Bureaucracy, suggest. At once a physical object and an abstract idea—an expanse within edges, variously permeable; an enormous sign, multiply read—it resists reduction in either direction: toward a nominalist language of material things ("Moroccan Agriculture is agriculture in Morocco") or a platonist one of ideal forms ("Indonesian Cooking is cooking with an Indonesian spirit"). Like any construction—a carpet, a bureaucracy, a field, a meal, or the efforts of a professional traveler to describe where he's been—it can be understood only by understanding how it is made out of what it is made out of, and what sort of uses it turns out to have.

c·ɔ

To choose the diffuse and unassertive "country" (Arabic, *blad*, Indonesian, *negeri*), rather than, as is much more common, such dense and freighted, and often enough tendentious, terms as "state" *(dawla, negara),* "nation" *(umma, bangsa),* "fatherland" *(waṭan, tanah air),* or "nation-state" (for which there is, for very good reasons, no unawkward equivalent in either language) to be the word behind the word for "Morocco" and "Indonesia," their deepest and most general referent, is more than an idle semantic move. It is to question the adequacy of the usual way of thinking about them, as infirm regimes dominating unformed peoples, and to suggest another: historical landscapes littered with politics.

What strikes one first about Indonesia (or anyway, as I wandered in the chaos of Jakarta's ministries, agencies, institutes, and police stations, struck me) is that it is a precipitate of the present, a pure product of collapsed colonialism, and about Morocco (gazing on Rabat's Ozymandian relics and their Arab-nouveau imitations) that it is an anachronism, a Renaissance princedom that has managed to last, through guile and good luck, into the twentieth century. What strikes one second (after an extended period beyond the charm of capitals) is that these judgments are false. And that leads one to a consideration of why so many analysts, indigenous and foreign, and indeed oneself, continue to be so strongly attracted to them. There are not many books on these countries as such (*Indonesia: The Possible Dream; Le Fellah Marocain: Défenseur du Trône; Revolt in Paradise; The Commander of the Faithful*) that do not see Indonesia as either fulfilling or betraying a popular revolution, and there are even fewer that do not see Morocco through the prism of its king. There is something in the way these places present themselves, to themselves and to others, as well as in the way we look at them and the hopes we have for them, that systematically misleads.

In part, this bias toward authority stories—the twists and turnings of unfinished revolution, the schemes and maneuverings of defensive monarchy—is an outgrowth of the troubled post-colonial history in the two countries. Regional revolts, urban riots, failed assassinations, near-miss coups (airport murders and shot-up picnics) coming one upon another, as well as reckless, first-time plunges (the Green March, the Malaysian Confrontation) into international politics, have led to an intense concern by just about everyone, outsiders trying to interfere, insiders trying to cope, not just as to whether the center can hold, but of what, in fact, the center consists. If (as is supposed) the state drives the country, what (are we to imagine) drives the state?

But there is more involved than the desire to read tomorrow's headlines today, and perhaps rewrite them. The notion that so much (in fact, nearly everything) depends on the passing melodramas of visible politics—who has the king's ear? (and what is it worth?), where are the Revolution's deliverers? (and what plans are they laying?)—grows out of a deeper mistake, even more obscuring: the disconnection of power from the conditions of its generation or the immediacies of its application, until it becomes a unitary, abstract force, defined, like glamour, magic, or the popular idea of electricity, solely by its effects. Elites monopolize it, masses are deprived of it; centers wield it, peripheries resist it; authorities brandish it, subjects hide from it. But what it is remains mysterious.

It will remain mysterious as long as the only questions asked about it are where does it lie and against whom is it directed, the fixations at once of both the right, concerned to shore it up, and the left, concerned to displace it somewhere else, rather than what, besides office, arms, and the exercise of will, brings it to life. The assemblage, over eleven centuries, of Morocco's cloud of tribal chiefs and urban notables, religious jurists and itinerant merchants, descendants of the Prophet and charismatic folk heroes, into an enormous labyrinth of personal loyalties, rivalries, conspiracies, and betrayals, and Indonesia's enfoldment, over fifteen centuries, of a vast conglomeration of peoples, communities, faiths, languages, habitudes, and lifeways into an ideological superculture have more to tell us about the nature of these countries than do Leviathan tales or stories of the shifting fortunes of political celebrities. States are as composite, as locally constructed, and as distinct as literatures, and at least as original.

Morocco, once one looks beyond its absolutistic self-presentation, is (and always has been) less a monopole despotism than an irregular field of micro-polities, small, smaller, and smaller yet, stretching out across the micro-environments—mountains, steppes, plateaus, littorals, deserts, oases, piedmonts, and alluvial plains—of the broken countryside, and reaching into its narrowest and most intimate social corners: families, neighborhoods, markets, tribes. Immediate, one-on-one, bargained-out dependency relations between personal acquaintances, what is sometimes called patronage, sometimes clientage, and by the Moroccans ṣedq (which means at once "loyalty," "trustworthiness," "friendship," and "truth"), lie at the base of things. What larger connectivities are achieved are brought about by establishing similar relations, similarly immediate, over broader and broader ranges of action.

In Indonesia, divided into islands rather than landscapes, the units are (and always have been), on the contrary, peoples—*suku, suku-bangsa*—the connective medium an ideology of general identity, and the country a would-be nation of nations. Javanese, Achenese, Dyaks, Dani; Muslims, Hindus, Christians; Malays, Chinese, Papuans—these are what need there to be joined. And what is needed to join them is a story that convinces them that they belong, by fate and nature, politically together.

Yet: what do we talk about when we talk about difference? To organize an analysis, or perhaps it is only an evocation, a story about places, around a global contrast, even one so glaring and durable as this *ṣedq* and *suku* one—a country held together, to the degree it is held together, by stretched-out webs of private loyalty and another held together, hardly more securely, by abstract ideologies of cultural unity—is to raise the suspicion that had other poles been chosen, other oppositions been set, other phenomena would have swum into view and other conclusions would have been drawn. And so they would have. And, if the oppositions were well chosen and their deployment careful, they would have their interest.

But there is a difference between a difference and a dichotomy. The first is a comparison and it relates; the second is a severance and it isolates. The dissimilitudes of Morocco and Indonesia do not separate them into absolute types, the sociological equivalent of natural kinds; they reflect back and forth upon one another, mutually framing, reciprocally clarifying. Or so they seem to do for me. I learned more about Indonesia when, shaken by the disturbances of the mid-sixties, I decided it the better part of valor to work in Morocco, than I would have had I gone back then directly to Indonesia. And I learned more about Morocco when, after things had settled down again in the seventies, I returned, not without trepidation, to Indonesia, than I would have by confining myself, as, beginning to find my feet in another civilization, I was tempted to do, thenceforth to North Africa. Tacking back and forth, between societies, histories, cultures, states, looking first one way, then the other, is how I formed my view of what these countries, as countries, come to. It seems only natural, therefore, and candid, thus to present them. Counter-cases, counterposed.

Why is it, then, this to-and-fro way of seeing things for the occasion granted, that such lately formed but early outlined countries as these, places that have been places ("The Most Distant West," "The Lands Below the Winds") for anyway a thousand years, but centered, or half-centered, polities ("Al-Makzan," "Le Protectorat du Maroc," "Al-Mamlakat Al-Maġribiya," "Mataram," "Oost Indië," "Republik Indonesia") for, at best, a few hundred, seem to show, wherever you cut into them along this chopped-up line of time, a certain character, reminiscent and completive of what you think went on before and initiative and presageful of what you see as having come along after? Why, through so many changes, so abrupt and thoroughgoing—overthrowings of dynasty, explosions of trade, invasions of foreigners, transformations of technology, alterations of faith—do they display, somehow, a perduring aspect even the most emancipatory and present-minded of citizens, bent on development, modernity, and the repudiation of tradition, can, however much it maddens them ("why, oh why, do we *never* change?"), hardly avoid seeing? We are all too familiar with this sort of thing in better-chronicled societies—England, Elizabeth I and II; Japan, Tokugawa and Present-Day—where the sheer continuity of history, its gaps walled up by polymath savants and specialistic scholars with endless detail, seems to us sufficiently to account for it. Finding it in less well chronicled ones, where the curve of fact is less easily smoothed, suggests that there is a good deal more to it than that.

The continuity, to the degree that it exists, is a continuity not of event, an improbable chain of ambiguous causes, nor of essence, a fixed innerness drifting through time. It is a continuity of political task: in Morocco, building up something that looks like governance out of locally anchored personal loyalties; in Indonesia, building it up out of diverse and rivalrous collective identities. From the time (the early eleventh century and the late twelfth) when the Almoravids and Almohads, gathering adherents and dividing opponents, moved out of the compacted palmeries of the pre-Sahara and the narrow valleys of the anti-Atlas northward to the Atlantic plains, the Mediterranean, and Andalusia, or when Majapahit (in the 1300s) claimed spiritual ascendency over a sixth of Asia from the thread-like river basins of northeast Java, either country has been a field of provincialisms sporadically expansive. No matter when you look, or where, what you find in Morocco is regionally generated movements, advancing, retreating, or hanging on; what you find in Indonesia is culturally discrete communities, aggrandizing, dwindling, or warding off. What lasts, or anyway has for a long time lasted, is not what it is these countries are. They are still terrains on which ambitions cross. What lasts is what it is they are up against: diversity, dispersion, and the enormous tenacity of immediate allegiance—to individuals, the force of character, in the one case; to we-ness, the force of likeness, in the other.

‿ꜱ

One can, again, cut in just about anywhere in the political genealogy of Morocco and Indonesia and see this contrast between a politics of *ṣedq,* the play of personages, most of them emphatic and virtually all of them male, and a politics of *suku,* the play of peoples, variously responsive to attempts to engulf them in larger wholes—in the period before the imposition of European rule, when all was rivalry and scatteration; during the Protectorate's or the Netherlands East Indies' delusory heydays, when enclave modernity and racial hierarchy seemed, at least to the ascendant, and at least for a while, right, natural, clear, and permanent; or after their replacement, with the planifications, investment policies, aid packages, and airlines of the modern state. In 1520, 1925, or 1986, the machinery is different, and so are at least some of the uses to which it is put. But not, or not so much, the emotions which drive it.

In Morocco in 1520 (to take for a starting point a year far enough back to qualify as traditional and far enough forward to seem ancestral to the present) there was a dying tribal dynasty in Fez, undermined within the city by sectarian divisions among religious figures and outside it by a chain reaction of adventurer breakaways. In the inter-mountain south, there was a gathering Sufi movement, whose leaders, having gained control of the caravan and slave trade with the Sudan and declared themselves Restorers, Saints, and Descendants of the Prophet, were headed north, first to Marrakech, ultimately to Fez, and finally to their own treacheries and fallings-out. Portuguese (and Genoese) traffickers were dug in in dark presidios, provisioned from the sea, along the Atlantic coast; Spanish (and Genoese) ones were dug in, a bit less claustrally, along the Mediterranean. Ottoman mercenaries, attached to one and then another local pretender, were pressing in from the Algerian east. A religious city-state was pushing, for the most part futilely, against the Christians in the northern hills. Armed ascetics, enveloped in sacredness, the famous marabouts, were striking out from fortified sanctuaries scattered through the Atlases, the Rif, the steppes, and the high plateaus. And in the eastern pre-Sahara, amid the relics of Sijilmassa, the legendary desert emporium that once connected Cairo to Timbuktu, there were the first faint stirrings of what was to become, a century and a half further on, the present monarchy, the Alawites.

This degree of political dispersion, in a country which is, at best, a thousand kilometers long and half that wide, set off in Californian seclusion by mountains, deserts, barrens, and seas, and, despite its micro-environmental diversity (also rather Californian), not all that poorly interconnected, is admittedly a bit extreme, even for Morocco. But not very much. The mid-seventeenth century, the late eighteenth, and the early twentieth look hardly different—only the weaponry changes. The picture of a cloud of assertive somebodies, rural and urban, religious and military, mercantile and hereditary, schooled and popular, settled and peripatetic, piecing together opportune coalitions and but partially, momentarily, and unevenly succeeding is thematical. And not only of the past.

Even after the beginning of the eighteenth century, when the Alawite dynasty, by then in Meknes, its first encastlement, organizes something that starts to look like a professional army, or the middle of the nineteenth, when, drawn at last into the diplomacies of Fez, it organizes something that starts to look like a proper administrative staff, the basis of power remains personal, brittle, situational, and dispersed. To the Europeans, now increasingly the English and French, enamored of legitimacy, centralism, and the line of command, this looked like Moorish decadence, an Oriental corruption of natural order, and an excellent excuse to intervene (which they were in any case doing) and put things right.

They had trouble enough doing it. Between 1900 and the middle twenties, dozens of battles (hundreds if you count the skirmishes), bloody, irregular, and hand-to-hand, were fought under the command of that horseback-romantic, "the royalist who [gave] an empire to [a] Republic," Colonel, then General, then Marshal,

Lyautey—in the desert around Figuig, in the mountains behind Khenifra, back of the coast at Casablanca, on the plains before Marrakech, and most spectacularly in the two sieges of Fez and the Riffian uprising of Abdelkrim—before the Protectorate, in either its French or Spanish versions, amounted to very much as a preponderant force. Even then, the *Présence européenne* was mostly just that: another set of would-be personages, lesser Lyauteys, amid a field of indigenous ones with connections of their own and no particular reason to believe in appointed authority and impersonal government.

The artificiality of the Protectorate, presiding, socially aloof and culturally intramural, from the small hill in Rabat called, like an attendant ministry to a foreign court, La Résidence, as well as its brevity (though formally begun in 1912 and formally ended in 1956, it was hardly in general control of things before the early twenties and was reduced to spectatorship by Vichy and the allied invasions by the middle forties), meant that any departure it induced from the brittle personalism of Moroccan society was local, partial, surface, and short-lived. It also meant that, unlike many colonial enterprises—India, Egypt, Indonesia, Mexico—it was not first established against the resistance of archaic power, frozen and traditionalistic, and only subsequently undermined, some centuries on, by the rise of ideologically driven social movements. Products alike of the 1920s and 1930s, improving imperialism and populist nationalism arrived together, flourished together, and weakened together. Both the dissolution of the Protectorate and the disintegration of the mass-based political organizations that arose to confront it began with their foundation. Ascendant for the moment, and only in favorable locations among selected populations, neither, in the end, ever really took hold.

In 1925, when Lyautey, having broken either the last of the marabouts or the first of the nationalists, Abdelkrim, finally departed, he left behind him, as he himself said, a task accomplished and a situation saved. Very large-scale, and, for the period, very highly rationalized, capital-intensive French farms (they may have been the most advanced in the world) had become established in the well-watered northern and central plains, what Lyautey called *le Maroc utile,* and an alliance between the prosperous *colons* who owned them and an enormously inflated corps of *mis-en-valeur* European officials (three times as many as the British needed to dominate India) Lyautey had put in place seemed about to fasten itself on the country and turn it into a proper *possession,* properly governed, properly stratified, properly understood, and properly exploited. But it was, as Jacques Berque, who was one of those officials, has called it, a *faux apogée.* Within a decade the alliance was shaken by the crash, within two it was shackled by the war, and within three it was trapped in an end-game hanging-on.

The political order that emerged when the end-game ended and the hanging-on took on a different, world-economy form turned out to be neither the Arabo-Muslim one-party state envisaged by the Islamicist wing of the nationalist movement, which dreamed of scriptural fidelity, moral unity, and religious awakening, nor the people's republic envisaged by the secularist wing, which dreamed of central planning, technical revolution, and *rive gauche* modernity. It turned out to be the revival (more accurately, the continuance, for, save in pockets, and those artificial, it had never really gone away) of the play of *şedq:* immediate and bargained dependency relations. Both these wings were in fact themselves so composed—ascending coalitions of local personalities, joined and divided by translocal ambitions. And so were the various traditionalists, tribal caids, and brotherhood sheikhs seeking to continue Lyauteyism by other means, who opposed them.

That the Alawite king should come to be again the most prominent figure in this swarm of figures was not inevitable. Without Muhammed V's exile and return by the French toward the close of the independence struggle, he would surely have been more directly contested. Nor, once monarcho-mania died with Muhammed V, was that prominence anything more than a relative matter. The monarchy was less restored—it, too, had never really been away, just immured in the Résidence—than the king was freed to do again what, if with other means, to other purposes, and in a less money-driven environment, his predecessors had always done: collect allies, find out rivals, and join the fray.

The efforts of Hassan II to do this, to find his feet in the politics of *ṣedq* as they extend to their widest range of connection, have been unremitting. Having no laurels to rest on, not even the history of his dynasty, the glory of his father, or the charisma of his office, though they help a little and are used when they are usable, there has been nothing for it but to work continuously to manage his relationships, not to doctrines and structures and publics, but to persons and situations and loyalties.

In the fifties, when he was still crown prince, it was the displaced notables of the old Spanish zone and a whole series of rebellious tribal strongmen in the north, east, and south of the country. In the sixties, after his accession, it was various sorts of nationalist heroes. In the seventies it was seditious soldiers. In the eighties it was yet other soldiers, urban intellectuals, and Muslim fundamentalists. The king has had continuously to struggle not so much to maintain his position as to establish it in the first place in a field of negotiated allegiance. "Henceforth," he told the country at what must have been his lowest point so far, after the execution (so it is rumored, with the king's bare hands) of his closest aide and army chief of staff for complicity in the 1971 attempt to kill him, "Henceforth I must never place my trust in anyone." But of course, like everyone else, however betrayed, he has. And, now that he's past sixty, he is teaching the art to his son, who will have, as he did, to do it all over again (in some ways, mostly material, from a stronger position, in some, mostly moral, a weaker one) if the monarchy, which is license to practice not a lump of power, is to survive. *Ṣedq* is sovereign.

In Indonesia in 1520, or thereabouts, the north coast trading states of Java, some old, most new, all trying desperately to expand, were one by one turning officially Islamic. The Portuguese, having invented the carrack and captured Malacca, had reached the Moluccas to confront its "islands full of kings and spices." A Muslim

sultanate, rich and bellicose, had been founded at Aceh, the west-
ernmost tip of Sumatra. A sea-rover state, not yet Islamic, not yet
Makassar, had begun to reach out from the southern Celebes.
Elsewhere there were dying Indic kingdoms—Hindu-Buddhist, as
they are usually called—in interior Java and defiant ones in sheltered south Bali. There were rivermouth trading towns, most of
them Muslim, in southern Malaya, the northern Celebes, northern
and eastern Borneo, and the southern Philippines. There were
hermetical tribes, most of them pagan, in inland Sumatra, Borneo,
the Celebes, and the bypassed islands of the eastern archipelago.
A scattered accumulation of sharply distinctive, deeply idiosyn-
cratic places, some of them drawn toward the sea, toward risk,
rivalry, money, and ethnic mélange, some hiding themselves, de-
fensively, in jungles, uplands, or sheltered inlets.

Here, too, then, the sixteenth century, the last one before European power becomes paramount in the archipelago, is in many
ways the hinge between the medieval and the modern. It was then
that the country became predominantly Islamic. It was then that
outsiders—Arabs, Indians, Chinese, Portuguese, Spaniards—began to stream in larger and larger numbers into the port cities that
lined the great sea street that runs from the Malacca Straits in the
west, through the Java Sea, to the pocket oceans—Banda, Timor,
Arafura—in the east. And it was then that those cities, each ruled,
to the degree they were ruled, by a local sultan or raja jacked up
from tribal chieftain, struggled with one another for regional pre-
dominance: Aceh, Malacca, and Johore in the west; Banten, Cheri-
bon, Demak, Jepara, Tuban, and Gresik in the center; Ternate,
Tidore, Ambon, and Makassar in the east. A great trade emporium
(which, of course, reached past the archipelago to the mainland
and the Philippines) both linked peoples together, and, in linking
them, dramatized their disconnections.

But long distance, overseas commodity trade is no more
confined to the sixteenth century than upstarts and marabouts are
in Morocco. As a Dutch historian famously put it, such trade is
"an historical constant" in Indonesia; rather like the climate. It
played an important role in the Indianization of a large part of the

archipelago, from perhaps the fifth century. In the seventeenth, it attracted the Dutch East India Company, then the greatest trading company in the world, in search of pepper, nutmeg, cloves, and sappanwood. It was central to the organization of the plantation colony (sugar, coffee, tobacco, rubber, tea) the Dutch organized, in the nineteenth and twentieth centuries, when the Company was no more. And it continues today, when exports, now of course for the most part industrial (oil, timber, bauxite, tin), international, and managed from Jakarta, account for nearly a fifth of national income, to be the heart of a good many matters. But more than the mere constancy of its presence is the constancy, or at least the durability, of its effect: to reinforce the in any case intense regionality of the country.

It not only has reinforced this regionality, rather than, as might be expected given the cosmopolitanizing view usually taken of trade, countered it; it has also reinforced, rather than countered, the extremely unbalanced shape of it. Today, ethnic Javanese account for about half the country's population, leaving the remainder divided among seven or eight moderately large groups and literally hundreds of small ones—a core and periphery pattern that seems to have obtained through much of the archipelago's history.

The great florescence of Indic civilization—Barabudur, batik, gamelan music, the shadow-play—occurred in Java. The sixteenth-century trade emporium was centered on its north coast, even if the most profitable cargoes came from elsewhere. The Dutch settled the headquarters, first of their Company, then of their colony, there. The rise of nationalism and the revolution against the Dutch mostly took place there. And today Java and the Javanese remain, despite strenuous efforts by the government to cloud the fact and occasional efforts, occasionally violent, by non-Javanese to alter it, the axis upon which the national life of the country turns. The Javanese contrast of *Jawa* and *Seberang* ("across," "facing," "opposite") may be an oversimplification of a more complex pattern, as well as a parochial view: folk categories usually are. But it does catch the effective look of things: folk categories usually do.

Indonesian nationalists have always regarded this situation as a heritage of colonialism, the result of a deliberate, divide-and-rule tearing apart of an ancient unity. But it is rather more the effect of the impact of an integrate-and-manage mercantile imperialism upon an ancient fragmentation. If the French were obliged to "pacify" Morocco sheikh by sheikh, the Dutch were obliged to gather up the East Indies people by people, fighting a series of extremely bitter and in some cases extended ethnic wars: against the Ambonese, Ternatens, and Gowans in the seventeenth century; against the Javanese in the seventeenth, eighteenth, and nineteenth centuries; against the Minangkabau in the 1830s; against the Achenese from 1873 to 1904; against the Bugis, the Balinese, the Torajans, and various smaller groups in the first decade of the present century. In unifying the archipelago under their hegemony, a process which took about two hundred years, the Dutch turned a competitive diversity in which Java was prominent into a hierarchical one in which it was preeminent.

By 1925, when the Netherlands East Indies reached its *faux apogée,* this Java-and-the-others structure of ethnic identification was locked thoroughly in place. Only northeast Sumatra, where tobacco and rubber growing were concentrated (and half the laborers were indentured Javanese), approached Java as a locus for Dutch attention, Dutch presence, and the billiards, whist, fans, and *rijsttafel* form of life that the planters, soldiers, and civil servants who lived it called *indisch.* With nearly two hundred sugar factories, again probably the most advanced in the world, planting eight or nine hundred hectares each (a tenth of the arable land) and employing about four thousand Europeans and Indo-Europeans and, at the height of the harvest drive, perhaps three-quarters of a million Javanese, plus dozens of Dutch-owned, native-worked tea and coffee plantations, the cultural, political, and demographic disproportion between Java and the rest of the archipelago was immense, awkward, and seemingly permanent.

Nationalism, too, despite the fact that a number of its leading figures were transplanted Minangkabaus from West Sumatra (who, in any case, soon lost out in the power struggles that followed

Independence) found its main battleground in Java and its champions mainly among the Javanese. The chief of these was, of course, Sukarno, the schoolteacher's son who emerged as a firebrand in the twenties, was more or less contained (for a period, literally) by the Dutch in the Depression, reemerged under Japanese patronage during the occupation, and became the Republic's hero-president in the revolution which followed. Here, there *was* a mass movement, a mass leader, and a mass emotion that lasted long enough into Independence, fifteen or twenty years, to set the terms—populism, struggle, unity, and revolution—of political discourse; terms which, however differently understood, some say twisted, some say purified, continue to prevail now that both the movement and its leader (one is not sure about the emotion) have left the scene.

The massacres of 1965 were also, of course, for the most part a Javanese, indeed an intra-Javanese, phenomenon; a conflict not between peoples but within one people, as to the symbolic basis, Islamic, Javanist, Civic, or Populist, on which "Java" and "The Seberang" were to be held together. Since then the history of the Republic has been broken, by the Indonesians themselves and by foreign observers following them, into the "Old Order" under Sukarno, a time of romantic nationalism, leftward drift, and final catastrophe, and the "New Order" under Suharto, a time of army domination, managerial rule, and seeming permanence. But whatever the differences in style, tone, policy, and technique of the two leaders, and whatever the contrasts in esprit or efficiency of the regimes they put in place, the continuity between them is a good deal greater than partisans of either would like to admit.

The continuity is again one of political task, here the collection into a single order of diverse peoples upon whom the larger causalities of history—not only trade or colonial domination, but religion (Islam, Catholic and Protestant Christianity, Hinduism, Buddhism), development (education, health, communications, urbanization), and ideology (nationalism, Marxism, liberalism, traditionalism)—have unevenly fallen. It is not simply the multiplicity of groups, cultures, languages, races, and social structures, but the depth of their disparities—in size, in centrality, in setting, in wealth, in complexity, and in world view—that insures that the politics of *suku,* the reconciliation of communities to one another, all of them to Java, and Java to itself, will remain at the heart of government. What Sukarno sought to do with rhetoric, charisma, and the mystique of revolution, Suharto has sought to do with soldiers, technocracy, and a ritual commemoration of revolution—to contain the divisiveness of cultural difference, pride, rivalry, and weight.

Suharto may have been the more successful: at least he has so far not so dramatically failed. But if so it has been by forging ideological instruments and coercive institutions to replace ardor, flourish, and exhortation. The revamping of Sukarno's largely declamatory and deeply Javanistic "Five Points," the *Pancasila,* into an officially ordered and officially enforced civil religion, the construction of an integralist state party, and the turning of the army (now perhaps eighty percent Javanese) into an all-purpose political tool has enabled Suharto, again so far, to achieve what his predecessor could only envision: the diffusion of Javanism beyond Java, the blurring of difference, and the containment of dissent. Suharto too, over seventy, is well along toward finishing his run. Whoever (or whatever) will succeed him is unclear. But whoever (or whatever), they will still be faced with a gatheration of peoples imperfectly balanced.

⌒

All politics is quarrel, and power is the ordering such quarrel sorts out: that much is general. What is not general is the nature of the quarrel or the shape of the ordering.

It is, of course, true that group rivalry plays a role in Moroccan politics, or any other, and that personal dependencies play one in Indonesian, or any other. What differs is the significance such matters, and others (wealth, pedigree, education, luck, allure, piety, access to weapons), which also appear in some form or other virtually everywhere, have in any particular instance: their salience, centrality, moment, weight. This is, as any player very soon realizes, an extraordinarily difficult matter to assess, which is perhaps why we social scientists, who are not players but reasoners and onlookers, professional second-guessers, are so given to abstract representations of Power, the State, Domination, and Authority—the drum-roll words of spectator realism.

The problem with such a no-nonsense approach to things, one which extracts the general from the particular and then sets the particular aside as detail, illustration, background, or qualification, is that it leaves us helpless in the face of the very difference we need to explore. Either we assimilate it to a system of abstract subtypes, of which there threatens to be no end (New Order Indonesia has been called, among other things, a patrimonial, a bureaucratic, a military, a post-colonial, a comprador, a repressive developmentalist, a neo-traditional, and a neo-capitalist state), or we regard it as superficial local coloring of deeper generic form (Moroccan or Arabic, or Islamic, or Middle Eastern, or Oriental, "authoritarianism"), or we merely ignore it as ambient noise—external interference with a readable signal. That does indeed simplify matters. It is less certain that it clarifies them.

Whatever price, and there is one, one pays in directness, surety, or the look of science by refusing to sequester politics from the specificities of the life in which it is embodied is more than made up for by the breadth of analysis that then becomes possible. The radical personalism of Moroccan politics extends beyond it into virtually every aspect of Moroccan life—into markets, law, kinship, religion. Or, one can as well assert, theirs extend into it. The same is true of the Indonesian attempt to reconcile group diversity and national unity. To depict power as some sort of featureless, universal force producing an abstract, invariant relationship called "domination" is to block perception of both the texture of politics and its reach, and leave us with hardly anything to say but that big fish eat little ones, the weak go to the wall, power tends to corrupt, uneasy lies the head, and master and man need one another to exist: the dim banalities of theory.

The politics of a country lie everywhere within it, not just in the institutions, this monarchy or that republic, by which, for the moment, they are more or less focused and somewhat organized. And though they change they do so at the speed the country changes, not that at which leaders, policies, or even regimes do. This is a hard lesson to learn in an environment so full of blare and alteration as contemporary Morocco or contemporary Indonesia. But it has to be learned if one is to understand what all the shouting is about; what sort of quarrel is going on. This is made in some ways rather easier, and in some rather harder, for the anthropologist who finds himself locked in a dense network of *ṣedq* dependencies in a disheveled town in central Morocco or engulfed by emphatic *suku* symbology in a shaken one in central Java.

3

Cultures

*O*nce upon a time, not so very long ago, when the West was a good deal more sure of itself, of what it was, and what it wasn't, the concept of culture had a firm design and a definite edge. At first, global and evolutionary, it simply marked the West, rational, historical, progressive, devotional, off from the Non-West, superstitious, static, archaic, magical. Later, when, for a host of reasons, ethical, political, and wistfully scientific, this seemed too crude, and too candid, the need for a more exact, more celebratory representation of the world elsewhere came into being, and the concept shifted to the life-way-of-a-people form familiar to us now. Islands, tribes, communities, nations, civilizations . . . eventually classes, regions, ethnic groups, minorities, youth (in South Africa, even races, in India, even sects) . . . had cultures: manners of doing things, distinct and characteristic, one apiece. Like most powerful ideas in the human sciences, this notion came under attack virtually as soon as it was articulated; the clearer the articulation, the more intense the attack. Questions rained down, and continue to rain down, on the very idea of a cultural scheme. Questions about the coherence of life-ways, the degree to which they form connected wholes. Questions about their homogeneity, the degree to which everyone in a tribe, a community, or even a family (to say nothing of a nation or a civilization) shares similar beliefs, practices, habits, feelings. Questions about discreteness, the possibility of specifying where one culture, say the Hispanic, leaves off and the next, say the Amerindian, begins. Questions about continuity and change, objectivity and proof, determinism and relativism, uniqueness and generalization, description and explanation, consensus and conflict, otherness and commensurability—and about the sheer possibility of anyone, insider or outsider, grasping so vast a thing as an entire way of life and finding the words to describe it. Anthropology, or anyway the sort that studies cultures, proceeds amid charges of irrelevance, bias, illusion, and impracticability.

But it proceeds. No matter how much one trains one's attention on the supposedly hard facts of social existence, who owns the means of production, who has the guns, the dossiers, or the newspapers, the supposedly soft facts of that existence, what do people imagine human life to be all about, how do they think one ought to live, what grounds belief, legitimizes punishment, sustains hope, or accounts for loss, crowd in to disturb simple pictures of might, desire, calculation, and interest. Everyone, everywhere and at all times, seems to live in a sense-suffused world, to be the product of what the Indonesian scholar Taufik Abdullah has nicely called a history of notion-formation. Bent on certitude, Olympianism, or codifiable method, or simply anxious to pursue a cause, one can ignore such facts, obscure them, or pronounce them forceless. But they do not thereby go away. Whatever the infirmities of the concept of "culture" ("cultures," "cultural forms" . . .) there is nothing for it but to persist in spite of them. Tone deafness, willed or congenital, and however belligerent, will not do.

When I began my work in the early fifties, the "they have a culture out there and your job is to come back to tell us what it is" conception of the anthropological enterprise was only beginning to be questioned, and then largely from outside the field. By the time I moved on to North Africa, about a decade later, doubts had grown somewhat stronger, and a good deal more interior, but nothing really drastic had happened to the general mind-set of the field. Our paradigms, for both research and writing, were still various sorts of classic "people studies" (the Navajo, the Nuer, the Trobrianders, the Ifugaos, the Todas, the Talensi, the Kwakiutl, the

Tikopia), with a few "community studies" (Tepotzlan, Suya Mura, a bit later on Alcalá de la Sierra) beginning to appear in complex societies—Mexico, Japan, Spain. Faced with Java, upon which just about every would-be world civilization has had a transformational impact, Sinic, Indic, Mid-Eastern, Romance-European, Germanic-European, and with Morocco, Berber and Arab, African and Mediterranean, factious tribal and walled-in urban, the sense of having gone to sea in a skiff was reasonably immediate.

It did not in any case take long to become aware that they indeed do things differently elsewhere, and think about them otherwise, differently from the United States, otherwise than one-self, differently and otherwise from one another. And it took only a little while longer to realize that a conception of culture as a massive causal force shaping belief and behavior to an abstractable pattern—what has been called the cookie-cutter view—was not very useful either for investigating such matters or for conveying what one claimed to have come up with from having investigated them. Something a good deal less muscular is needed, something a good deal more reactive; quizzical, watchful, better attuned to hints, uncertainties, contingencies, and incompletions.

To make all this somewhat less programmatic, let me give just one example, compressed and illustrative, and preliminary to what I am going to have generally to say, of such reactive, "what is going on here?" cultural analysis in my own case.

The first thing one does when setting out to study a country such as Indonesia or Morocco, or a town therein, aside from reading various books, variously useful, is to begin to learn the language. That in itself, before one gets anywhere near systems of land tenure, rules of marriage, or ritual symbolism, suggests enough conjectures, however offhand, to project one imaginatively, however off-balanced, into the middle of things. You don't exactly penetrate another culture, as the masculinist image would have it. You put yourself in its way and it bodies forth and enmeshes you.

I began studying Indonesian about a year before going to the field. (It was a group, "aural/oral" effort together with my col-leagues, directed by a Malayo-Polynesian linguist—two in succession, actually—sent up from Yale and "informed" by a native speaker studying at Harvard.) Indonesian, a variety of Malay, is the national language of the country, but what then was spoken in Pare, and for the most part still is, was Javanese, a related but, say like French and Italian, different language. So, after arriving in the country, my wife and I spent another seven months studying that language in the old Javanese court town of Jogjakarta. We hired local college students to come to our hotel room one after the other, relay style, through the day, as instructors, and adapted the Indonesian lesson plans the linguist had prepared—that is, had our instructors translate into Javanese the Indonesian sentences that had previously been translated to English, and then speak them back to us.

As for Arabic, I began my engagement with it (not to use a stronger word) by taking a formal course in "classical"—that is, modern standard—while I was teaching at Chicago, supplementing that with, again, "aural/oral" work with a Moroccan graduate student from Fez on colloquial Moroccan, the language actually spoken, some Berber aside, in Sefrou. (The old Harvard sentences got translated once again, into bravura structures they had never dreamed of, and worked very well.) Later, my wife and I spent six months in Rabat, using local college students in dawn-to-dusk relay style as we had in Jogjakarta; and when we returned to Chicago we found yet another Moroccan graduate student to work with us. What is so often represented in anthropological texts, when it is represented at all, as an academic enterprise, a bit like getting on top of algebra or swatting up the history of the Roman Empire, was in fact a multi-sided, multi-languaged (Dutch and French, the colonial languages, were involved as well) social interaction, involving in the end—for the process continued after we arrived at our sites, where our initial encounters took the form, we supposed readily comprehensible, believable, and thus unthreatening, of language lessons—literally dozens of people.

A great many things that had nothing very directly to do with such properly linguistic processes as Javanese deixis or Arabic morphology, both of which are more than a little astonishing, were first brought toward the edge of awareness during the course of all this exchanging of multiply reworked, prefabricated sentences. But here I want to mention, and connect in an oblique and somewhat paradoxical way, merely two: the stress on status marking in Javanese and that on gender marking in Arabic. Or, more exactly, by Javanese and by Moroccans. For, whatever it was that Benjamin Whorf was trying to say, it is not the forms of language that generate meaning but, as Ludwig Wittgenstein did say, the use of such forms to think about something—in this case, who gets deference and what is the significance of sexual difference.

One of course assumes that with any people status discrimination and gender definition are going to be matters of some concern. What is of interest, and what varies, is the nature of the concern, the form it takes, and the depth of its intensity. That, in the cases at hand, we are facing not only a sharp difference in this regard, but something near to direct inversion, first came home to me when, in studying Javanese, my instructors insistently and meticulously corrected any errors I made (lots of them—there are lots of them to make) in status marking while letting gender errors more or less go, while my Moroccan instructors, like the Javanese, as university students, hardly traditionalists, never let a gender mistake (also lots of them and abundant opportunities to make them) pass uncorrected and seemed hardly interested in status marking, such of it as there was. It didn't seem to matter, or matter very much, whether you got sex right in Javanese (most of the time it was lexically neutralized) so long as you kept rank straight. In Moroccan, getting genders crossed seemed almost dangerous; certainly it made my teachers, all of them men, as indeed were the Javanese, very nervous. But rank hardly came into consideration at all.

The languages as such support these disparate tendencies to notice some things about the world rather more than others and to make more fuss about them. (Javanese has no inflections for gender, but is grammatically stratified into minutely graded, hierarchical speech registers. Moroccan Arabic has gender inflections for just about every part of speech, but no status forms at all.) But that is too complex, and too technical, to go into here. What is important here, in this classroom demonstration of what cultural analysis is and isn't, and how one finds oneself almost reflexively doing it, is what sort of conclusions about Moroccan and Javanese ways of being in the world these contrasting experiences, in their very contrasting, lead on to, what more substantial matters move into view.

It is not, in any case, the mere and simple fact that Javanese are preoccupied, as they are, with the giving and withholding of gestures of respect and that Moroccans have constructed, as they have, an ontological wall between the male and female halves of their population. The passing traveler, without the languages and with hardly more than guidebook knowledge will notice the head lowerings and the softened voices, the eye-slit veils and the concealed wives; and the inegalitarian aspects of Southeast Asian life, like the sexist ones of Mediterranean, have been noted by just about every writer who has attempted to describe them, sometimes to the virtual exclusion of anything else. Indeed, the tendency of such readily visible matters to encourage stereotyping, as well as a certain sort of easy moralizing, is one of the things that has brought the concept of culture, or again more precisely, the anthropological use of it to talk about peoples—the megalomanic Kwakiutl, the stalwart Nuer, the disciplined Japanese, the family-prisoned Southern Italians—into question.

What puzzles and sets one to meditating about the Javanese insistence on the errorless use of status markers and the Moroccan of gender ones (aside from surprise at the dusty corners, teaching language to a casually encountered foreigner, into which the general presumptions of a people reach: some aspects of culture apparently really *are* everywhere), is not so much their obvious contrast but, again, their anthropologically generated conjunction. It was I, after all, not my instructors, who happily corrected me to a single truth, upon whom the contrast fell; and considering the cases together, interpreting them in terms of one another—as reciprocal commentary, independent difference rhetorically connected—virtually forces you to wonder about the presence of the absent term. If the Javanese are not, as one very soon learns they are not, insouciant about sexual difference (the colloquial address terms for small children are "penis" and "vagina"), and Moroccans are not, as is even more readily evident, calmly oblivious of standing and reputation (the obsequiousness of petitioners is a crafted art), then the thought arises, almost of itself, that in the one place sexual difference gets expressed and understood as a domestic variety of status and that in the other inequalities in prestige get assimilated to the invidious imagery of sex.

Once you begin to look at, or listen to, things this way, you find, like a physicist with a new particle or a philologist with a new etymology, "evidence" (and "counter-evidence") everywhere. "Culture" gets polyphonic, even disharmonic, themes invoking counter-themes which reinvoke themes, instructively offset from the originals.

The facts that, traditionally at least, and in some families still, Javanese husbands speak to their wives in a status-lowering register and wives to their husbands in a status-raising one; that incest is regarded more as a status error, an inappropriate mixing of levels, than as an emotional crime, a confusion of intimacies; that genealogies begin with androgynous gods and descend, via duplicating identical twins, to humans through marriages of unidentical twins, then siblings, then first and second cousins—all lead one, as do a host of other things from the composition of village councils to the picturing of shadow-play figures, into a world where sexual identity exists as an inflection of social hierarchy.

The facts that Moroccan Muslims, at least traditionally and in some places still, regard Moroccan Jews as women (in pre-Protectorate times they could not carry guns), and often other foreigners—Tunisians, Egyptians, visiting anthropologists sent off to sit with the ladies—as well ("those Egyptians can't win," one of my informants said as the Six-Day War approached: "if they lose to the Jews everyone will say they were defeated by women, if they defeat them everyone will say 'all they did was beat a bunch of women'"); that the monarchy is drenched in masculinist symbology; that the discourse of both commerce and politics has a

persistent edge of seduction and resistance, flirtation and conquest—all lead one, as do a number of other things, from the
understanding of sainthood to the metaphorics of insult, into a
world where rank and station are sexually charged.

Even this reversed, dominant and subdominant representation
will not do, however. For what one discovers when one looks at
Java with Morocco as optic and the other way around is that one
is faced not with a collection of abstractable, easily stateable
themes (sex, status, boldness, modesty . . .) differently tied into
local bundles, the same notes set into different melodies. One is
faced with complex and contradictory fields of significative action,
most of it tacit, across which assertion and denial, celebration and
complaint, authority and resistance, continuously move. When
ingeniously juxtaposed, these fields can shed a certain amount of
light on one another; but they are neither variants of one another
nor expressions of some superfield that transcends them both.

And this is the case for everything, Moroccan refractoriness,
Javanese effacement, Javanese formality, Moroccan pragmatism,
Moroccan brusqueness, Javanese loquacity, Javanese patience, Moroccan haste (to list some other beckoning clichés getting myself
into things fairly quickly produced) with which you find yourself
faced as you try to make out what the people you are thrown
together with are on about. You are comparing incomparables; a
useful enterprise, and, when the stars are right, an informative one,
however illogical.

All this aside, and the example concluded, it is of course quite
definitely not the case (though the contrary is sometimes pre-
tended) that an adequate account of the workings of culture in
such world-historical places as these can be constructed on the
basis of personal interactions and immediate observations—listen-
ing, looking, visiting, and attending. Both countries, and both
towns within those countries, are ingredient in forms of life geographically very much wider and historically very much deeper
than those they themselves directly display. One cannot talk sen-
sibly about Moroccan (or Middle Atlas, or Sefroui) culture, or

about that of Indonesia (or Java, or Pare), without in the first case invoking such elusive, difficult to bound and impossible to encapsulate mega-entities as "the Mediterranean," "the Middle East," "Africa," "Arabs," "France," and "Islam," or, in the second, "Oceania," "Asia," "Hindu-Buddhism," "Malays," "the Dutch," and again, but with a somewhat different spin, "Islam." Without such ground, there is no figure, and what you see before you has hardly more meaning than a fire in the distance or a shout in the street.

Yet, how to manage this relation between the large and the little, scene-framing, background matters, which seem momentous, general, and historically fixed, and local goings-on, which do not, is far from clear. It has, in fact, proven increasingly troublesome to anthropologists since, mainly after the Second World War, they began to move away from tribal microcosms, or imagined such, toward societies with cities, creeds, machines, and documents. There has been much hesitation and more than a little evasion. Focused pictures have been hard to come by, and when come by crude and schematic.

That Indonesia and Morocco are, and have been for centuries, about sixteen in the one case, about twelve in the other, geographically peripheral members of two different, continuously interacting, occasionally interfusing, world civilizations—that which begins roughly at the Indus and ends, even more roughly, at the Moluccas and New Guinea, and that which, mapping things the other way, begins more or less at the Oxus and ends, conventionally, in the Western Sahara—is a primary fact about them. Their location at the outer edges of enormous cultural continents whose heartlands are elsewhere is something of which their peoples, however caught up in parochial concerns and however suspicious of outside influences, have been continuously aware. They have always been outliers, Farthest India, the Most Distant West, and they have always had the cultural devices, Hindu legends and Arabian poetics, Buddhist monuments and Persian gardens, Dutch furniture and French cafés, to prevent them from forgetting it.

The history of notion formation thus lives in the present, and culture as it manifests itself in this bazaar or that funeral, this sermon or that shadow play, in ideological division and political violence, city form and population movement, and in language learning, carries with it everywhere the marks of that fact. Understanding a form of life, or anyway some aspects of it to some degree, and convincing others that you have indeed done so, involves more than the assembly of telling particulars or the imposition of general narratives. It involves bringing figure and ground, the passing occasion and the long story, into coincident view.

☙

The recognition that there is, culturally, much in Indonesia and Pare, Morocco and Sefrou, that was not made in those places, that has not only its origins but its canonical setting somewhere else, is quickly come by. Views about how the rich ought to behave and the poor to be treated, about how the world came to be, how truth can be sorted (if it can be) from error, about what happens to people after they die, about what counts as attractive or repellent, impressive or tawdry, about what moves or amuses or leaves one cold, are (unlike countries, and unlike towns) difficult to localize in anything but a diffuse and unbordered way. But perhaps the most immediate of such reminders, especially again to someone trying to look in two places at once, is the cast of characters—not the individuals, though they are striking enough, but the *dramatis personae*—who appear, suitably named, coifed, and costumed, and even, it sometimes seems, with a good deal of their dialogue already scripted, before you.

People, as people, are doubtless much the same everywhere. That is what you commit yourself to in calling them people, rather than Egyptians, Buddhists, or speakers of Turkish. But the parts they play, the parts available for them to play, are not. There are no fellahs in Indonesia, though there are certainly people who work the land—they are called tanis—and suffer the afflictions (not altogether the same afflictions) that go along with doing so. There are no gurus in Morocco, though there are certainly people

who present themselves to their fellows as spiritual exemplars—
they are called siyyids or marabouts—and experience the quandaries (not precisely the same quandaries) that then arise. Even such
personae as appear in both places—hajj, for example, or sultan;
nowadays "newspaper columnist," "leftist," "financier," and "media personality"—come somehow to something somewhat different, classic characters on unclassical stages.

The matter is made even harder, for a now-and-then visitor
trying to follow the proceedings that, enacted by such characters,
unfold on such stages, by the fact that what is center and what
edge depends not only on what it is that looks but on what it is
that is looked toward, and what it is that is looked toward is wildly
various. Sefrou looks toward Fez. Fez looks toward the citied
Morocco of Rabat, Casablanca, Marrakech, Tetuan, and the rest.
Citied Morocco looks eastward toward Cairo, Baghdad, Teheran,
and the rest, as well as northward toward Madrid, Paris, and, more
than a bit ambivalently, pan-Mediterraneanized Marseilles. Pare
looks toward the high art court regions of Central Java. The court
regions look toward Jakarta, where Indonesia is supposed to be
summarized but perhaps is manufactured. Jakarta looks toward
Southern Asia and Northern Europe. And all, of course, look
toward the great centers of power in the modern world: Washington, Tokyo, Moscow, and New York. These cultural outliers have
. . . have had . . . for the foreseeable future will continue to have
. . . an enormous amount from which to be outlying.

Both Moroccans and Indonesians as such and Arabists, Indolo-
gists, Islamicists, Orientalists, and ethnographers, many of them,
themselves, by now Moroccans or Indonesians, have been more
than a little at odds concerning what to make of this situation: how
to view not only the involvement with faiths, sciences, arts, laws,
and moralities concocted elsewhere, but the tangled multiplicity
of such involvements. Some have tried to argue that a "local
genius" or a "primordial substratum"—Afro-Berber in Morocco,
Malayo-Polynesian in Indonesia—has been so strong as to render
importations incidental, so much foreign ornament easily stripped
away to reveal the indigenous authenticity concealed beneath. But

those who took them, later on by those observing those who took them, as neither surface nor sectarian, but foundational, allusive, deeply inwrought: "The Religion," indeed, of Java, and thus, *a fortiori,* of Indonesia. What has come to be known as indigenization" had set in.

By "indigenization" (*indigenisasi,* not precisely an indigenous term) is meant an attempt to deal with the problem posed to Koranic orthodoxy by plurality of belief and diversity of practice, and by the unwillingness of the "New Order" state to tolerate plurism, by defining all save what is clearly inassimilable, because explicitly Christian, pagan, Indic, Sinic, or unbelieving, as "Islamic." Most especially, it seeks to reduce the tension between the more observant and devotional and the more eclectic and experientialist elements of the population by redrawing the boundaries between what is and what is not admissibly Muslim—redefining what counts as observance, what qualifies as devotion.

The reification of that most capacious, pliable, manifold, and ill-defined of Muslim categories, "Sufism," into a creed-for-all-contexts dogmatical system, and the finding of it everywhere, high and low, past and present, liturgical and literary, have played an important part in this move toward religious lenience and the broad mosque. So have the rereading of traditional Javanist texts as locally encoded Muslim commentaries, the officialization of Islamic education, Islamic leadership, and even to some extent Islamic observance, and scholarly characterizations of Javanese kingdoms as "Sufi theocracies," Javanese palaces as "analogues of Mecca." Not orthodoxical veils over syncretical bases. Not sectarian factions battling with rivals. Rather, vernacular universalism. Spiritual singleness shining forth in a vast exuberance of homegrown forms.

This is not to say that indigenism is unchallenged, either as program or interpretation, any more than pluralism and separationism were and are. Reformists, traditionalists, secularists, syncretists, and that peculiarly Javanese persona, *ahli kabatinan,* perhaps least badly translated as "metasubjectivist," all remain, convinced and insistent, and both Middle Eastern shock waves and

such arguments have been fairly thoroughly discredited, both by ethnohistorical research and, even more, by colonial uses of them to undercut resident elites ("Arab" as against "Berber" in Morocco, "court" as against "village" in Indonesia) as themselves "un-native." The more common responses have been either to accept the fact of multiplicity and try somehow to give it a local, homegrown look, or to minimize it and privilege one or another ingredient in it as the heart of the matter. Or, of course and most often, both at once.

There are a large number of examples one could take to spell this incertitude succinctly out. But surely the best, at least right now, when everyone seems to have a view about it, usually confident, and it has reemerged as one of the declamatory categories of universal history, is (whatever it is) "Islam." Not only has the rise in Muslim self-consciousness, self-assertion, and self-dividedness pushed religious issues, and religious personae, more toward the center of things in both countries, but scholarly attention, once confined to a few specialists, experts on law, rite, or the evolution of brotherhoods, has, since Khomeini, Qaddafi, the murder of Sadat, the destruction of Lebanon, and the invasion of Kuwait, virtually exploded.

Indeed, the attention may, so far as Indonesia and Morocco are concerned, have grown more rapidly than the phenomenon itself. Whether or not either or both of these countries are becoming more thoroughly engulfed by the energies of Islam (a matter concerning which I, at least, am of several minds), the students of their cultures, foreign and indigenous, Muslim and non-Muslim, most certainly are. But a few years ago neglected as relic traditions worn down by modernity, the Quran, the Sharia, the Ayads, and Sufism now are invoked to explain just about everything.

Of the two cases, the Indonesian, and again most especially the Javanese, would appear at first glance to be the more complex. Islam came to the archipelago, gradually, segmentally, and more or less peaceably, via Persia, Gujerat, and the Malabar Coast, from about the fourteenth century, after more or less a millennium of

Hindu, Buddhist, and Hindu-Buddhist presence; a presence itself installed in what was apparently a diverse collection of long-in-place Malaysian societies, themselves anything but simple. Sorting out its place and significance in the texture of Indonesian culture has been, in result, a delicate matter, much contested.

Contested, again, both by scholars and by those the scholars were (and are) ostensibly studying. The two lines of discourse, that of those professionally dedicated to separating things out, on the way to reconnecting them in some other, more perspicuous way, and that of those existentially obligated to living their way through them, separated or unseparated, have in fact tended, and increasingly, to mirror one another, even to grow into one another. Common understandings of common times.

During the colonial period, and especially the closing phases of it when the rise of pan-Islamism, Reformism, and Muslim mass organizations persuaded the Dutch that they needed to have less a bookish than a behavioral knowledge of "Islam," the general view was that the Islamic impact on the archipelago, and particularly on Java, was a surface matter. The Creed of the Prophet (it was said), of which most Javanese (it was also said) had anyway but a dim and primitive comprehension, lay upon the island and its thoroughly Indicized culture "like a veil." It was a "religion," to which there was, indeed, some commitment, occasionally strong. But it had not penetrated very deeply into the substance of society, which remained pliant, indulgent, diffuse, and syncretic—ungiven to dogma, averse to conflict. A *de facto* God and Caesar separationism settled into place, not only, as one would expect, on the Dutch side but, with a few exceptions, defined as *fanatik* and nervously distanced, on the Javanese as well. The forms of Muslim learning and worship were set aside as "spiritual," thus "personal," "private," "inward," and "unworldly," and, their pursuit protected, left more or less to themselves. But collective actions in the name of Islam, being "secular," thus "political," "public," "external," and "worldly," were not and, carefully overseen, prudently self-restrained, were limited to moral and charitable, so-called social, matters.

With the rise of nationalism all this chan[ ] militants, separationists collaborators. And [ ] point at which I, unencumbered with eitl[ ] happened upon the scene), it disappeared [ ] and the political came, with emphasis, back t[ ] noisy and organized, became a force amon[ ] define the soul of the new society. By 1952,[ ] Islamicist and Indicist, populist and elitist, tr[ ] larist conceptions of what sort of country [ ] ought to be, what sort of culture it ought to[ ] into causes—fixed, distinct, jealous, and det[ ]

"Islam" at this period appeared less a star[ ] (or more exactly, for there were internal divisi[ ] a collection of movements), more thoroughly [ ] of society, mainly commercial, and in some [ ] mainly coastal, than in others, and bent on se[ ] over competing movements otherwise anim[ ] based. A pluralistic, conflictual view represen[ ] veil nor as bedrock but as a particular persuas[ ] others, hardly less absolute, thus seemed, bot[ ] with rising trepidation, and, so far as I could s[ ] uneasy *dramatis personae*—gurus and ulama[ ] party secretaries, implacable youths and [ ] whom I was talking, exact and veridical. I wa[ ] I wrote about all this *Religions in Java*. B[ ] believer, apparently, in ethnographical kinds,[ ] programmed audiences, wouldn't have it, and [ ] normalized and against its argument, as *The [ ]*

In any case, five years later events complet[ ] heavals of 1965 and the soldiers' peace that f[ ] the conception of the place of "Islam" in Indc[ ] most critically, in Javanese, began again to shif[ ] be a collection of spiritually driven politica[ ] movements being forbidden and in the wake c[ ] larly discredited, the Muslim interest became [ ] stances. Only now these stances were increasing[ ]

the state's imposition on the whole of the country of a Javanistic civil religion have complicated the picture more than a little. Nor is one obliged to conclude that there are no grounds for preferring one sort of account of the place of Islam in Indonesian or Javanese culture to another just because there are several on offer. Perhaps because I was involved in constructing it, but not only because I was involved in constructing it, I think the pluralist, field-of-differences view has force not only for the 1950s, but for the 1920s and the 1980s as well (and perhaps even more for the 1990s, as the contradictions of free-market authoritarianism begin to set in); that neither Islam as overlay nor Islam as immanence will in the end really do.

But that's as may be. The story, far from approaching end and resolution (what, after all, is six hundred years?), is but just begun. The history of notion formation, in this aspect of culture as in any other—and the story of "Islam" actually stands rather well as a patch sample for a general weave—is an obscure and unsettled process. Sorting out the domestic from the imported, the bred-in-the-bone from the lightly held, the dying out from the coming on, is a continuous business, carried on without much in the way of codifiable rule or systematized plan. It is concluded only when, at a loss for the moment as to what to say next, you turn, equally improvisationally, to another patch out of another weave.

The resolution I have taken, to this point privately, not to describe either of my cases as a reduced version of the other, the bane of a great deal of comparative analysis in the human sciences—Spain lacked Holland's Calvinism; China, Japan's feudality—becomes peculiarly hard to sustain when you look, as I, of course, did, at Islam in North Africa immediately after looking at it in Southeast Asia. Things that seem "missing," absent terms truly absent, fairly leap out at you.

In the first place, nothing comparable to a thousand years of Indic civilization faced the bearers of Islam when they arrived on the plains of what is now central Morocco toward the end of the eighth century. There were some Berber chiefdoms scattered about in the hills and some passage ports along the coasts. But the Roman presence, never that strong this far west, had, like the Phoenician that preceded it, long since disappeared, leaving behind little but a few mosaics, a handful of place names, and apparently, no less relic, some unusual Christians. Nor did anything much happen culturally to these Arabian adventurers—most were either marauders or refugees—as, with no Persia or India to spiritualize them in between, they made their way, in the space of months, along the southern shores of the Mediterranean.

In the second place, and in part as a result, there is nothing here, now or in the knowable past, comparable to the Indonesian mélange of ethno-spiritual groupings formed around religious or quasi-religious ideologies. Nor—Jews, never much more than an encapsulated percent or two of the population, in part aside—are there significant numbers of indigenous non-Muslims. Nor is there much in the way of ethnic or regional unevenness of Islamization, of concern with what is properly Islamic and what merely Arab, or of anxiety about the orthodoxy of local practice. And, perhaps most important, there is no mismatch between community of citizenship and that of faith. National identity and religious affinity seem sides of a coin. No need, here, for a thinned, officialized civil religion to convince people that their broadest political loyalties and their deepest spiritual ones are reconcilable.

But this is, indeed, beginning to sound a little like Henry James's "no Epsom, nor Ascot . . . no cathedrals, nor abbeys" view of Hawthorne's America. What is critical about Moroccan Islam is not that it doesn't much take, and hardly ever has much taken, the sort of associational, thought-streams form that Indonesian so often has. What is critical is the radically individuating, men-in-their-roles form (women are, again, divided out—dispatched to reticence and household piety) that, virtually whenever you look and where, it does take. Positively characterized, Islam in Morocco is sustained by personages, by a vast, inconstant crowd of severely independent, grand and middling, middling and petty, religious notables: scholars and judges, descendants of the Prophet and popular charismatics, brotherhood chiefs and Meccan pilgrims, prayer leaders and quranic lesson-givers, mosque officiants, mortmain administrators, and court notaries, law expounders, sermon givers, and supervisors of bazaar ethics. Alims, qadis, sherifs, marabouts, sheikhs, hajjis, imams, fqihs, talebs, nadirs, adels, muftis, khatibs, muhtasibs—like the society generally, an irregular network of irregular figures, constantly adjusting their plans and allegiances.

In seeking some order in this day-to-day, place-to-place, era-to-era play of personalities, some more emphatic, some less, but all concerned to make whatever they can out of whatever their religious positioning sets before them, scholars, and again, if less self-consciously, the personalities themselves, have tried to isolate some cultural fault lines, urban vs. rural, learned vs. popular, hereditarian vs. charismatic, most of them at least as old as Ibn Khaldun, with respect to which matters might be, ad hoc and somewhat, sorted out. Faced at any particular point and any particular location with a particular constellation of familiar types, neither arranged into hierarchical structures nor sorted into ideological camps, no clerical establishment, no *familles d'esprit,* what seems to be called for is seeing how the Islam of Islamic personages enters into the general scuffle of social life.

That general scuffle is, as I have already described it, a matter of the piling up and breaking down of shifting systems of alliance out of handshake loyalties—in itself a radically secular, pragmatical, dry-eyed matter, uninfected with transcendent concerns. What, as participants in that process, religious figures add to it, or more exactly, embed within it, is a strenuous, insistent, even aggressive moral tenor, the color of principle beyond the strategic. Nothing of much importance goes on, or, so far as I can see, ever has, in this in many ways so worldly society, free of the pressures of Muslim conviction, simply because nothing of much importance goes on, or ever has, free of the involvement of the alims, sheikhs, sherifs, marabouts, and the like, whose vocation it is to see to it that those pressures, as they severally conceive them, are not relaxed.

This moralization of social struggle by the presence within it of religious personalities possessed of one or another notion of what it is for a country, a community, an individual, or a state to be truly *mu'min* ("faithful," "believing," "upright," "honorable") is observable at all sorts of junctures and in all sorts of situations. The configuration of views concerning what it is that makes someone genuinely Muslim certainly changes, and will continue to do so. The propagation of those views by the deeds and dealings of impassioned men struggling for place, looks, like clientalism, to be rather more abiding.

In the, so it looks to us now, transitional sixteenth century, when Morocco began to take its modern shape, the competition among diverse and antagonistic religious figures is so prominent as to seem to drive the whole society. The emergence of rural ecstatics as social prophets; the multiplication and intensified combat, especially in the cities, among brotherhood sheikhs; the reassertion of descent from Muhammad as the founding principle of monarchic authority; the appearance, literally out of nowhere, of men calling themselves "Mahdi" or "Imam" (that is, divinely guided "restorers" and "rectifiers," messiahs Muslim style); and the reactive insistence against such explosions by scholars and legists, "the friends of the Sharia," of the supremacy of textual orthodoxy—all this fashioned the moral landscape, a scattered structure of determined opinion, within which the Morocco of the Alawis, of the Protectorate, and of the present developed.

As in the Indonesian case, and for similar reasons—the fall of the Shah, the rise of militancy—there is just now a good deal of scholarly reexamination, both domestic and foreign, of this whole process. Long-received ideas—the importance of Christian intrusion to the development of Moroccan nationalism; the political discontinuity between settled plains, subservient to government, and tribal mountains, resistant to it; the quasi-Caliphal role of the king; the quietist-reactionary role of the brotherhoods—are subject, again, to fierce debate, as is the weight overall of Muslim belief in Moroccan history. But whatever the outcome of the debates (which are tending, too, to take an "indigenist" direction) or the assessment of the force of Islam (no one now thinks it surface or secondary), the religion of personages, like the politics of private loyalties, persists undimmed.

എ

It is, I suspect, an experience every field anthropologist has, and certainly one I have had so repeatedly that I have come to think it emblematic of the whole operation, to come upon individuals in the course of research who seem to have been waiting there, at some unlikely place, for someone like you, bright-eyed, ignorant, obliging, credulous, to happen along, so as to have the chance not just to answer your questions but to instruct you as to which ones to ask: people with a story to tell, a view to unfold, an image to impart, a theory to argue, concerning what it is that they, their town or village, their country, their religion, their kinship system, their language, their past, their way of growing rice or bargaining or weaving, their music, their sex, their politics, their inner lives, "really," "genuinely," "truly"—*in fact*—are. *Sampeyan, kula ngomongi,* the Javanese say—"you, I talk at" (the verb is causative, not suasive, an impacting force); *šuf! nqūl-lek,* the Moroccans— "attend! I say unto you" (the mood is imperative, almost quranic).

Anthropologists react diversely to such persons, and the same anthropologist reacts diversely to them at diverse times. Sometimes they seem lapel-grabbers, essential to escape from, so we can see things, as we like to say, for ourselves. Sometimes they seem like natural deposits of raw expertise luckily stumbled upon: great informants make great anthropologists. But whatever one's reactions, and however vacillating, it occurs at length, or anyway it has occurred to me, after the fact, in that double punned meaning I have been so shamelessly exploiting here, that the "you, I talk at," "attend! I say unto you," stance is one's own. I, too, have stories to tell, views to unfold, images to impart, theories to argue, and am eager to expose them to whoever might sit still and listen. To describe a culture, or as I have here, selected bits, purposively arranged and cut to fit, is not to set out some odd sort of object, a knot in hyperspace. It is to try to induce somebody somewhere to look at some things as I have been induced, by journeys, books, witnessings, and conversations, to look at them: to take an interest.

This notion, that to describe a form of life is to show it forth in a certain light, nicely adjusted, seems harmless enough, even banal. But it has some difficult implications, of which perhaps the most difficult is that the light, such as it is, and the adjustment as well, comes from the description, not from what the description describes—Islam, gender, speech style, rank. Things are, doubtless, whatever they are: what else could they be? But it is in accounts of them that we traffic, our informants', our colleagues', our fore-runners', our own, and they are constructs. Stories about stories, views about views.

Just why this idea, that cultural description is fashioned knowl-edge, second hand, so bothers some people is not entirely clear to me. Perhaps it has something to do with the necessity, if one adopts it, of taking personal responsibility for the cogency of what one says or writes, because one has, after all, said or written it, rather than displacing that responsibility onto "reality," "nature," "the world," or some other vague and capacious reservoir of incontaminate truth. Perhaps it is the result of a fear that to acknowledge that one has put something together rather than found it glistening on a beach is to undermine its claim to true being and actuality. But a chair is culturally (historically, so-cially . . .) constructed, a product of acting persons informed by notions not wholly their own, yet you can sit in it, it can be well made or ill, and it cannot, at least in the present state of the art, be made out of water or—this for those haunted by "idealism"—thought into existence. Or perhaps it is merely that accepting the fact that facts are made (as etymology—*factum, factus, facere*—in itself ought to alert us) plunges one into the sort of laborious, winding, and nervously self-conscious tracing of how one has come to say what one has come to say that I have tried to begin, for my own case, here. The flat presentation of bankable findings does indeed seem simpler and more straightforward, comforting, knowledge as it is supposed to look. The only trouble is that it is, itself, a bit of a romance, and not altogether the most artless one.

Two disrupted towns, two half-ordered countries, two conglomerate forms of life, and a recurrent anthropologist building collapsible airships do not make for sharp conclusions. What they make for, or so I hope, is an instructive example of the heuristic uses of belatedly appreciated commotion and muddle, the value there is in coming too late and leaving too early, in drifting along, like an earnest excursionist, behind the partial sightings of receding experience.

4

Hegemonies

One remembers in many of the classical ethnographies a snapshot of the anthropologist standing among "his" natives. Usually he is in the center of the picture, frequently but not inevitably taller than those, almost always men, gathered around him, all looking stiffly toward the camera, he dressed in white, or some camping uniform, often with a pith helmet, sometimes with a beard, they in some sort of native dress, normally simple, sometimes with a weapon; and usually, too, there is some sort of landscape in the background, jungle, desert, shambling huts, perhaps some goats or cows, suggesting remoteness, isolation, self-sufficiency. There were variations: the ethnographer writing notes by the light of an oil lamp, questioning a man hoeing in a garden, sharing a water pipe, lounging in a longhouse; or sometimes there was merely a native holding up a spear or calabash ("is this what you want?"), looking toward the ethnographer, visibly invisible behind the camera. Where there was no such picture, the topos was in one way or another, in a preface, a footnote, an appendix, an aside, somehow conveyed: a man, on occasion a woman, more or less like ourselves, only braver, isolated, far out and far away, among people, not only not like ourselves, but disconnected from us, visited, observed, reported upon. The ends of the earth.

This sort of presentation of the anthropologist as a lonely explorer at the world's edge, far from the madding crowd, hardly appears anymore. It is not just that it is a bit much, now that our ideas about "primitives" have grown less primitive and our sureties about "civilization" less sure: the very notion of "among the Dangs" isolation lacks, these days, much application. There are very few places (now that gold panners have discovered the Amazon and New Guinea has discovered the political party, there may not be any) where the noises of the all-over present are not heard, and most anthropologists work by now in places—India, Japan, Bolivia, Egypt . . . Indonesia . . . Morocco—where such noises all but drown out local harmonics. Nor do they work alone, save for a missionary or two, an itinerant district officer, or the odd castaway; masters of all they can survey. The woods (or the deserts) are full of sociologists and philologists, economists and historians, musicologists, agronomists, psychiatrists, tourists. It is possible to exaggerate the difference. The "down deep in the jungle, far out on an atoll" image was always a bit concocted, the signs of other foreign presences besides that of the ethnographer rather carefully painted out, and there have always been those who worked in Hong Kong or Hollywood. But it is difficult to exaggerate its significance for, to borrow an idiom not my own, the social conditions of ethnographic production. The movement of anthropologists into societies rather more consequential in the flow of world history and the migration into that flow of the more peripheral societies on which, "in search of the primitive," we previously concentrated—both the result of the political repositionings following World War II—altered not just what we study or even how we study it. It altered the medium in which we exist.

To convey this, what it is to be an anthropologist not off somewhere beyond the reach of headlines but on some sort of fault line between the large and the little, photographs are quite inadequate. There is nothing to picture. So too are prefaces and appendices. They marginalize what is central. What is needed, or anyway must serve, is tableaus, anecdotes, parables, tales: mini-narratives with the narrator in them.

It is dawn, four-thirty or five A.M., early in October 1957. My wife and I are living with a Brahmana family, traditionally declining, moderningly coming on, in southwest Bali. Once appointed clergy to the local court, ritual officiants to lords and kings, they no longer have a high priest or the prospect of producing one. The father, who formerly would have had his youth expended being trained for ordination, is an itinerant barber, and reputedly a clumsy one. The sons are in school hoping to be civil servants, though they will end up hotelkeepers. The daughters, also in school, are studying to become something Bali has hardly had before: box-office-oriented professional dancers. (A decade hence I will see them perform—with their father as their agent, reputedly a shrewd one—before perhaps a thousand people in a Chicago convention hall.)

We have been awakened by the awareness that our small courtyard is packed with fifty or sixty Balinese men. They are just standing there, motionless and silent, in ordered rows, dressed for work in the rice terraces. I get out of bed, fearing the worst. Accusation? Protest? Physical attack? These are tense times. Sukarno, angered over the New Guinea issue, is getting ready to expel the Dutch whole and entire. Civil war threatens in Sumatra and the Celebes. A European doctor has been murdered with a field hoe by his Balinese assistant. Most foreigners have left or, in the case of some expatriate painters who have been there for decades and are married to Balinese, have been forced to leave the island. But I'm unable to imagine what could possibly have brought on this confrontment. We have been working on irrigation weirs, village markets, ice manufacturers, and tooth-filing rituals. Hardly the stuff of quarrel and suspicion.

When I get outside, people begin murmuring, "You ask him," "No, you ask him," gently nudging one another forward. An elderly man finally takes a half-step toward me. Gesturing obeisance, he says, in a voice so soft I can barely hear it: "Please excuse us, 'father' [I am thirty-one, he somewhere between fifty and eighty], but we have a question to ask. RRI [the state radio] says the Russians have put a moon up in the sky. But the RRI is run by the government, so we don't know. Is it true?" I say (my source being the BBC World Service, in which my confidence is absolute—I am counting on it to tell me when to run): "Yes, they have. It's up there, spinning around, right now." Various people then nod to one another and say: "If an American admits it about the Russians, it must be so," and, the old man begging my leave with grand elaboration and apologizing again for having dared to disturb me, the crowd floats back into the morning haze. Empiricism in action. Intercultural communication professionally effected. The Cold War in real time.

Seven years later, in 1964, I am driving desperately about Morocco, trying to make what is the most fateful decision—short of flight— an ethnographer faces: where to set up shop. I have, in fact, more or less decided on Sefrou from an earlier reconnaissance, even more breathless—twenty-one towns in thirty-five days. The Pasha is affable, my children can live there in reasonable comfort, and there are Berbers, Jews, olives, and walls. But I want to take another turn through a half-dozen of the more interesting places, just to be sure. And also, I suppose, to persuade myself, so that later on I can persuade others, that I am doing things scientifically. First you conduct a survey, then you take a sample, and finally, weighing probability and payoff with Baysean prudence, you make a selection.

Qsar al-Kebir, the last place I visit, is not, as a matter of fact, really a candidate. A sprawling, unprepossessing place, fifty kilometers back from the Atlantic coast, just inside what was, until 1956, the border of the Spanish sector of the Protectorate, and subject to enormous, mud-soaked floods, it is far too large, far too unhealthy, and far too close, for my traditionalist tastes, to the harlequin atmospherics of Tangiers. But, centered around an old, decaying Spanish presidio that, complete with an uncannily Hooverish tower, looks like a small-scale version of Stanford University, it was the scene of a famous sixteenth-century battle in which the Moroccans repelled a Portuguese invasion, discouraged an Ottoman one, and lost a famous leader, and so it intrigues, especially since the first time through it was largely under water and I was unable to find anyone useful to talk to.

This time I do. He is Hassan ben Ali, the Pasha of the place, who looks like Vladimir Nabokov (everything here seems to remind me of something else), but turns out to be the grandson of one of Old Morocco's more colorful characters: "Emily, the Shareefa of Wazan." Emily was an Englishwoman who, in 1873, at the age of twenty, married the sheikh (he was perhaps fifty) of one of the most powerful and seclusive religious brotherhoods in the country. (She met him at a Tangiers musical soiree; he divorced two Moroccan wives, by whom he had already produced his legitimate heirs, in order to marry her; and their wedding, opposed by both families, featured a white-faced chestnut horse caparisoned in gold lace, a contingent of cheering British sailors on leave from a flag-showing gunboat at anchor in the harbor, dressy honor guards from every legation in Tangiers, the Moroccan Administrator of Customs *cum* Delegate of the Sultan, and crowds of "Moors" pushing rudely by her to kiss the hem of her husband's cloak.)

The brotherhood, lodges of which are found all over Morocco, was founded in the seventeenth century in the suspicious, closed-in mountain town of the western Rif, Wezzan, whose life and spirit it continues to dominate. Its members regard themselves as descendants of the Prophet by a more direct line than that of the ruling monarchy, with which their relations over the centuries have been, to put it delicately, complicated. Emily herself lived mostly in Tangiers, presiding, as "Madame de Wazan," over a circle of European consuls, expatriate literati, and German princesses, and traveling to Wezzan, where she felt surrounded by intrigue (accurately enough—she nearly got poisoned), only now and then. Two of her husband's older sons went mad, to a large extent from drink, and the other predeceased him. In time, their marriage foundered (he sold off her property, married a servant, disfavored her family), but she gave him two more sons and remained with him to his rather messy end. One of these sons had in turn twin sons. One of the twins died in childhood. It is the other, fat, squat, blotched, and virtually immobile—he is sixty-three, and looks exhausted—I now am facing.

He is living alone in Qsar in an enormous, dark, shabby-genteel commandante's house, furnished in the Hispanico-Moroccan style of sixty years ago and crowded like a provincial museum with curios from Tunisia, Egypt, Lebanon, Syria, Iraq, and the Gulf, in the center of the crumbling and otherwise unoccupied presidio. He begins, because I ask him to, by discussing his political career. (He speaks idiomatic English.) He was the chief intermediary between the monarchy and the invading Americans at Port Lyautey/Kenitra in 1942. He was one of the few high officials who remained loyal to Muhammad V during his exile to Madagascar in 1953 and was himself house-arrested to Fez. Since Independence, he has been Pasha in three or four towns, each more provincial—he has his enemies—than the last. But suddenly he breaks off and, apropos of nothing, launches, for two uninterrupted, monological hours (enormous plates of food, produced by an ancient servant summoned with a foot-bell, keep appearing, one after another) into a curious tale that seems inversely to recapitulate, or perhaps to parody—the second time farce—the history of his grandmother.

While at Port Lyautey he met and fell in love with the wife of an American naval lieutenant. The French disapproved of the liaison (what they actually disapproved of, and wished to undermine, was his go-between activities at their political expense), and they prevailed upon the Americans to ship the lieutenant and his wife home. But this didn't work, anymore than—his comparison—the exile of the king did later on. The woman left her husband (he was her fifth or so, so it wasn't much of a wrench) and returned to Hassan, and, though, like his grandfather, he already had a wife and children, he—unlike his grandfather—married her polygamously.

Unfortunately she turned out to be a raging alcoholic and kept having what he called, slipping into the more gendered French, *crises*. But he was blinded by love for her. Even though she slapped his face, threatened to kill him, and disappeared with other men for days at a time, he remained with her. Finally, however, she pushed him over the edge, by demonstratively leaving their hotel one evening in Fez with a Jew and returning with him, equally demonstratively, the following morning. He told her that he could accept anything but an insult to his sherifian honor, and threw her out. What he called her "guardian," some sort of relative I suppose, presently arrived from the United States. There was a prolonged, cross-cultural, and cross-religious legal struggle and a grand scandal. But a divorce was finally effected and she went back—where else?—to Boston. After Independence, she wrote to him, pleading to be taken back. But, though he still loved her, and always will, he refused saying that you couldn't have plural wives anymore in Morocco. (That is, he couldn't, socially. Legally it was, and is, of course still possible.) She then proposed that she come back as his mistress. He said no, people of my standing can't get away with that anymore either in this day and age. By now she has gone more or less totally to pot. The last he heard she was in either an insane asylum or a house of prostitution. He is not certain which, or how much difference there is, actually, between the one and the other.

This cultural echo chamber, collecting *vieux maroc,* Spanish, French, English, and *en passant,* American imperialism, Independence, nationalism, and *jeune maroc,* social and sexual cosmopolitanism, religious and political insularity, male narcissism, Middle Eastern style, female adventure, Euro-American style, into a story with little plot and less moral, leaves one, or anyway left me, feeling that an enormous amount of enormous importance has been said without being sure just what it is or why it is, to me, a drop-in motorist on an indefinite errand, right now being said. Past and Present. Orient and Occident. Self and Other. Desire and Domination. How much we say, as Hofmannsthal says, in saying "twilight."

Let me now reverse locales—to Sumatra; move back in time—to 1958; and heighten drama—to civil war. My wife and I, she desperately ill, for a while we think mortally, with infectious hepatitis,

I, only slightly less desperately, with malaria,
curious case of iatrogenic myopia that mispres
have brought on, are in Padang, a small, ill-she
the island's precarious West Coast. We have com
theory that the comparison of a strongly Muslim
kabau, of which Padang is, such as it is, the i
strongly Christian one (Minahassa, in the northei
we intend to go next) with Hindu Bali (where w
will deepen our understanding of the complex
spirituality.

I suppose it might have, but our timing is off.
arrival a regionalist rebellion that has been brev
so but that everybody assumes, as they assume
looks inevitable, will never actually happen ("The
thing out; they always do") finally breaks out.
the rebel headquarters. The insurgent governm
our hotel; its military command is just down
government warships appear, like ocean sentriei
bor. Sukarno is in Tokyo, where, ailing and
spends a lot of time these days, and there is an ey
pause while the country awaits his return. The
he will disguise a deal in a blur of words an
avoided. (All the rebels seem to want is a cabi
God knows he has done that often enough.) H
evening and gives, practically upon descent fi
extraordinary speech that puts paid to that i
huddled over a radio, on our veranda with a
breathing young Minangkabaus. (They have c
sign in English saying "Up and Down with Hu:
the rebel army. In my one intervention in Indon
them they haven't quite got it right.) He is
direct, above all resolute: pronounces an ana
blockade, threatens an invasion. The Minang
reality dawning. The next morning the warshi
foreign vessels attempting to enter the port
others already there from leaving, sandbags are

otel and along the waterfront, guarded by machine guns and
tillery, and there are a couple of air raid alarms. We are, it seems,
randed.

The next two months are a badly plotted adventure movie—
ght to a mountain town when the situation in Padang grows
ore threatening; flight from it, when it begins to be bombed by
e central government, across the vast tropical forest of Central
umatra . . . strafed roads, shuffling refugees, bombed-out river
ridges . . . to a rebel controlled oil camp on the eastern coast
here my wife, still too weak to walk, can get proper medical
tention; the capture of the camp by central government para-
oopers dropping soundlessly from the morning sky—the details
which can be left aside. What is odd (and seemed odd then) is
ow surrounded at every point this seemingly deep-Indonesia
xperience was with the diffracted presence of the United States
America. No matter how far you get away from some things,
parently, they are, like debts, embarrassments, failures, or child-
ood, always there.

One of the reasons the United States was, in this derivative and
usive, scattered-out way, "there" was that, as everyone, myself
cluded, assumed at the time, it was more than a little implicated
the whole affair. The rebellion, and the suppression of the
bellion (for it was in the end crushed), were Indonesian affairs,
oduced by Indonesian rivalries, justified by Indonesian notions,
d carried out by Indonesian instruments; but American fishing
troubled waters—this was, after all, the heyday of John Foster
ulles, for whom no quarrel was too remote, no conflict too petty
long as it rang with echoes of anti-Communism—was . . . how
all I put it? . . . significant. American arms shipments to the
bels were rumored, CIA machinators were said to be running
ound somewhere machinating, Dulles made Dullesian noises
out recognizing the rebel government, and a number of singular
ents—a drop of guns manufactured in Michigan near a Suma-
n airbase, the shooting down of an American pilot flying a rebel
mber in East Indonesia, various smugglings of American goods
m Chiang's Taiwan—kept the U.S. ambassador in Jakarta busy

issuing explanations, denials, apologies, and reassurances. To be in rebel territory just then was, however inadvertently come about, hardly, for an American, an innocent business. Some causes you join; others join you. God knows who those students thought I really was.

There was one American already in Padang when we arrived— the head of a United States Information Service library—but he soon fled, or was evacuated (he was vague on the matter; clear only that we could not go out with him), leaving his brand-new automobile hidden in the woods nearby and asking us to get it out when we left. He didn't suggest how we might do this, but in any case it can't have been all that well hidden: when we thought to use it to flee ourselves it wasn't there. Soon after his departure, a dozen or so American media types showed up and camped for a few days in the hotel. (I was by then so disoriented that I asked one of them what "CBS" stood for.) But they soon grew bored because "nothing was happening" and they couldn't get any rebel leaders, by now concealed in the woods themselves, to interview, so they returned, in the same mysterious way they had come— there are blockades, and there are blockades—to Jakarta. (Ever the helpful anthropologist, I tried to tell them a bit about the society that was rebelling—one of the few in the world both Muslim and matrilineal—but they were uninterested.) In the United States, my mother phoned the State Department. They told her that as they had not heard anything about us for more than a month, they could only assume that we were dead.

The emanations from home, in any case, kept coming. When we fled from Padang to the mountain town, we arrived there in the middle of its first air raid, conducted, none too effectively, by three circling Mitchell bombers of a sort I had not seen since being transported in one during World War II. The oil camp to which we then fled was operated by an American company, Caltex, in a lease arrangement with the Indonesian government, which of course could not now get at it, nor could anyone get out. A mid-America suburb in the jungle (bungalows, lawns, some of them—would you believe it?—artificially watered, curved streets, a supermarket suffused with muzak country music, a gymnasium and a canteen similarly suffused, that modern clinic we were headed for), it was largely populated by roustabout Texans whose views of Indonesians of any variety tended to be dim, and by terrified rebel troops (they kept firing howitzers at monkeys) deployed along its edges. When the central government, determined to get the oil flowing and back in its hands, finally invaded from the air, the first civilian plane allowed to land was that carrying Caltex's General Director for Indonesia. When it returned the next day to Jakarta to pick up the Vice Director we were on it.

But perhaps the oddest of these unaddressed postcards from America, certainly the most baffling—to this day, I'm not entirely sure the whole thing wasn't a malarial dream—arrived earlier on, the evening we were preparing to leave Padang. All foreigners, except our doctor, a World War II German army surgeon working for the rebels, and the owner of our hotel, an ancient German-Jewish lady who had fled Hitler in the late thirties (the two were the best of friends, chattering drunkenly of Europe late into the night), had long since left. The city was virtually deserted as people, fearful of the shelling which in fact began a few days later, drifted back to their villages. Packing our things—a few clothes, a lot of fieldnotes—we were startled to see an American in a camouflage suit emerging from the jungle a hundred yards away. He marched up to us and announced that he was the American vice consul from Singapore. What he was doing there, how he got there, and how he had found out about us he didn't say. What he did say was that he had been instructed to inform us that as we had gotten ourselves into the fix we were in (we had never thought otherwise) the United States government assumed absolutely no responsibility of any kind for us (we had never imagined that it would). He then turned around and marched back into the jungle. A Great Power, come and gone. So much for the American Century.

Another encounter with a somewhat different America (Ronald Reagan's) in a quite different place (a Marrakech resort hotel) at a much later point in my progression (the winter of 1985) was rather more social comedy than political melodrama: minor Anthony Powell, not downscale André Malraux. But it was, in its way, no less memorable.

I was invited (I remain uncertain why) by the Aspen Institute for Humanistic Studies and the Moroccan-American Foundation, two institutions with which I had not previously had any connection, to a conference on, no less, "Morocco: Past, Present, and Future," chaired by the Honorable Charles H. Percy, chairman, until a few months before, when, much to his surprise, he was not reelected, of the Senate Foreign Relations Committee, and the Moroccan Foreign Minister, His Excellency Abdelatif Filali. Among the thirty or so other participants, guests, observers, and whatnot were the executive vice president of Citibank; the vice governor of the Bank of Morocco; the vice president of Johnson and Johnson International; a former American ambassador to Senegal; Jimmy Carter's ambassador to Morocco, now chairman of the United States-Japan Foundation; our current ambassador to Morocco; the head of the United States Information Service; a general partner in something mysterious in Wyoming called Kendrick Cattle Company; the chairman of something even more mysterious in Manhattan called Golightly-Harbridge, Inc.; the director of the Royal College in Rabat; the chancellor of Pace University in New York; the vice chairman, and also a recently unseated senator, of Capitol Bank in Washington; the managing director of "The Institute of International Finance" (a Frenchman); the president of "Association Internationale Futuribles" (a Moroccan); the curator of the Neiman Foundation, until recently the managing editor of the *Washington Post;* the foreign affairs columnist of the *New York Times;* the director general of the Moroccan Customs Administration in Casablanca; the director of the Islamic Conference Trade Center, also in Casablanca; the secretary-general of the Moroccan Ministry of Planning; the chairman of AB Volvo, Gothenburg, Sweden; yet another recently unseated senator, this one of Arab descent; a former French foreign minister, born, as he kept reminding us, in Morocco; the prime minister of

Morocco; and M. le Baron Guy de Rothschild, "Rothschild, Inc., New York, New York." I had, apparently, rather come up in the world.

The discussions, which went on, morning and afternoon, mostly in English, occasionally in French, only once or twice in Arabic, for five days—one day on financial policy, one on technology, one on "the interaction of political and social processes," and so on— were really rather incidental to the occasion, which had to do with more important things than ideas. Except for Senator Percy, who, outmaneuvered, found himself stranded in the chair while his counterpart worked the corridors, most of the grander figures appeared only sporadically at the conference as such, concentrating their attention on the series of elaborate lunches, dinners, and cocktail parties held at various sites around the city, and some never came at all. (The Moroccan prime minister appeared only once, striding in, totally unexpected by anyone, at the head of a retinue of twenty attendants, on the afternoon of, appropriately enough, the "interaction of political and social processes" day, smack in the middle, it so happened, of my talk, which, even more appropriately, was on the fluidity, personalism, and arbitrariness of power relations in the Moroccan state. Dumbfounded like everybody else, I just sat down, as the prime minister went around the room vigorously shaking everyone's hand. He then gave a short address—in French—on Moroccan-American friendship, went around the room again shaking everyone's hand, and strode out, his people following. I then tried to finish my talk. But I had rather lost my audience: no need to tell what has just been shown.)

The discussions, in any case, were largely an exchange of First World exhortations and Third World excuses. The Americans, nothing if not righteous, urged radical Reaganomics—deregulation, the market, reduction of public expenditures, tax breaks, friendliness toward foreign investment, reality, and strength of character—upon the Moroccans. The Moroccans, defensive and put-upon, urged appreciation for Morocco's vulnerabilities—its colonial past, the oil shock, deteriorating exchange rates, EEC trade discrimination, poverty, ignorance, weather, and the complexities of Arabic—upon the Americans. The French sided substantively with the Americans and rhetorically with the Moroccans, a nice pirouette. Except for fatigue, some agenda-making (a *lot* of agenda-making), and a certain amount of moral annoyance, nothing much happened.

That is, again, in the sessions: it was the social goings-on, intense and intricate, surrounding the sessions that gave shape to things. The Moroccan contingent were furious with their head, whom most of them regarded as an American toady and a bit of a climber, for permitting a fiery Moroccan feminist who was not an invited guest to join the company—this at the behest of Senator Percy's wife who complained that there was only one woman in "their" party. (There were none in "ours," though most people brought their wives.) The American contingent were uneasy not only about the fact that their prominent figures flew first class in the same plane as the less prominent flew economy, and were put up in a more splendid hotel, a half-mile away, but even more by the fact that the only black, who, as a former ambassador, should properly have been sorted with the elite, was put with the masses both in the plane and in the hotel. The presence of a number of young French women lounging around the pool in topless bathing suits, massaging and being massaged by young French men, upset the Americans, especially the women. (I am unsure what the Moroccan reaction was—I couldn't get them to talk about it—but they could hardly have found so brilliant an example of neo-colonialism unembarrassing.) But it was the momentous question that hung over the entire conference, not answered until its very end, but discussed throughout as though both success and honor depended upon it—Would we be granted an audience with the king?—that most colored the whole affair, and that, when finally answered, with a half-affirmative, left it in fluster and disarray.

The news that we would be received came at the last moment as we were back in our rooms packing to leave. Buses would come in an hour to take us to the new palace the king had just constructed as an expression of the movement of the country's center of gravity southward now that he had gone into the Sahara. (He was, in fact, in Marrakech mainly to celebrate the tenth anniversary of his doing so, to establish the city as a symbolic co-capital with Rabat, and had summoned from Rabat all foreign ambassadors, a dozen or so, who had arrived within the year, to present their credentials. We were an afterthought.)

But a hitch appeared. The women, both the Moroccans and the Americans, who had spent the hour frantically dressing themselves up for the event (most of the Moroccan ones, wives of the partici- pants, emerged into visibility for the first time), were informed, after they had boarded the bus and contrary to what that hapless head of the Moroccan contingent had assured them earlier, that they would not be received. Amid much bitterness, directed by the Moroccans toward the head and by the Americans toward the king, Islam, Arabs, "this bloody country," and the Middle East, and some soul-searching among the American men, which didn't take long, as to whether they should go, the women descended from the bus. (*Lèse majesté* is no archaism here: the king refuses, he is not refused; certainly not by defrocked senators.) The rest of us took off for the palace leaving the women standing, as chagrined as they were angry, in the hotel driveway.

The comedy, however, was not yet over. When we arrived at the palace, a neo-Moroccan Arabian Nights affair, the enormous gates were closed behind us as we paraded in (and the ambassadors paraded out) past desert-costumed attendants in long, serried ranks. The audience itself took place in an enormous chamber, empty except for a mountain of fruit piled on a table in the center. The audience as such was routine enough. We were each intro- duced to the king, who seemed tired but affable, stood around talking to him, and to one another, for an hour or so about nothing much, save our goodwill and his appreciation of our goodwill, and then left past the same attendants through the same gates. Outside we found, the one forlorn, the other steaming, the American ambassador to Morocco, a rather pallid man in any case, and, a new figure on the scene, in no way pallid, the American ambassa- dor to the United Nations, General Vernon Walters. Walters had just flown in, I assume for the occasion, from New York. His plane was late and the two arrived at the palace just as the gates were closing behind us. The guards, who had their orders, refused to reopen them, so the distinguished guests did not get to be guests and were obliged to cool their heels in the forecourt and, like the shut-out women, missed the party. The intercourse of nations, if that's what all this was, apparently operates no less strangely between kings and ambassadors than it does between consuls and ethnographers. In diplomacy, as in most things, there is a home court advantage.

Back again in time, to the summer of 1971, across again in space, to the north-northwestern tip of Sumatra: a place called Aceh. By general repute the most passionately Islamic region of Indonesia— "Mecca's veranda"—as well the most obstreperous, having engaged the Dutch in their longest and most bitter colonial war from 1873 to 1903, having rebelled against the new Republic, partly on ethnic, partly on religious grounds, in the nineteen fifties, and continuing to the nineties to be a site of violent resistance, sporadic and obscurely motivated, to state authority, it is not the easiest society for an outsider, white, Western, and (thus) presumptively Christian, to navigate.

I had come there in yet another capacity, new to me and not since repeated: I was a technical consultant, hired by a wealthy American philanthropic institution, if not absolutely the wealthiest, certainly the most active and the most famous, to advise it as to how, how much, and upon whom to spend some of its money. The Ford Foundation, which had a field office in Jakarta, wished to raise the level of Indonesian social science research (that is, by Indonesians, in Indonesia, on Indonesian problems, as opposed to bringing people to the United States to study, which had turned out to be both very expensive and a mixed success), and I was dispatched to travel about the country to see what might be done. In the space of a couple of months, I visited a dozen or so universities, of varying degrees of seriousness and reality, in Sumatra, Java, Bali, and the Celebes, after which I retreated to Vermont and wrote a report recommending the setting up of a series of small and dispersed regional research stations for the practical training of field investigators. Rather to my surprise, as it was an against-the-grain idea in bureaucratized, big-project Indonesia, not only was the recommendation accepted and put into practice but the stations flourished.

Moving about not as an ethnographical scholar looking for customs to collect but as a foreign aid expert trying to give money away rather changes your relation to people, theirs to you, and yours to yourself. This was especially true in Aceh, which, unlike Java and Bali and even the Celebes, was, given its reputation for belligerence, bigotry, backwardness, and xenophobia, not used to being attended to by would-be benefactors from industrial places. It was an encounter of innocents. I did not know what I was supposed to do. The Acehnese did not know what to do with me. And neither of us knew whether importing thought from Harvard or Chicago was altogether a good idea.

When one doesn't know what to do, one, of course, does everything. I was plunged, and plunged myself, into a hectic social round. I was escorted to see an artificial mountain of whitewashed concrete built by a seventeenth-century sultan so that his wife, who was from what is now southern Vietnam, would not long for the hills of her homeland. I was taken to an enormous graveyard where hundreds of Dutch casualties of the Acehnese war, generals among them, lay buried. I attended an elaborate wedding in which clashing images—shawled heads and slit skirts, chanted prayers and popular music, Muslim judges and foreign guests—charged the air with enormous tension. I gave a talk to the economics faculty on agricultural development and another to the law faculty on customary law; was taken by an incredibly zealous Australian, Tasmanian actually, convert to Islam (he thought the Acehnese lax) to a number of new government-sponsored schools for the teaching of government-sponsored Islam; inspected the new air-conditioned library the state oil monopoly, soon to go bankrupt in Indonesia's most famous scandal, had built for the university; and journeyed with the modernist, and rather dispirited, governor of the province to the traditional village where he was born and to which he was about to retire. I attended a meeting of the regional development commission, a collection of foreign-trained technocrats from Jakarta putting together a five-year plan, looked at a gigantic, Near Eastern–style mosque being constructed in the capital by the central government, visited a copra plantation along the coast, got a clandestine tour of a haven for smugglers tucked away in the tip of the island, and was given an official goodbye dinner, complete with speeches and avowals of friendship, in a refurbished sultan's palace.

All this in the course of a week. The superficiality was exhausting. It was far more exhausting than the day in, day out, one step forward, one step back, effort to get genuinely close to a handful of people who have no particular reason to get close to you that field anthropology normally involves, and I spent what energies I had left trying to escape, if only for some hours, into the everyday world, the one in which Acehnese existed as moral realities for one another, that I knew was there, and indeed could see, filling the streets and fields, as I passed through it en route to some official handshake or other.

The means to such escape came via my known interest, for I had written on the subject fairly extensively, in the traditional religious boarding schools in Indonesia called *pesantren.* These schools consist, most commonly, of a number of young men in their teens or twenties, who live in a complex of simple dormitories, sheds, really, set round a mosque, also simple, in which, for a number of hours each day, they study various religious texts— quran, hadith, devotional tracts—under the general direction of the scholar, usually a Meccan pilgrim, in charge of the mosque. The students come and go more or less as they wish, obtain and prepare their own food, work part time to maintain themselves, and eventually return to their villages, sometimes setting up their own *pesantren.* In recent years, there has been a good deal of effort to "modernize" this pattern, reduce its casualness, and connect it more closely to the state system of formal schooling. But it remains strong, and nowhere more than in Aceh, where it is the generative core of deep Islam, the primary place where faith is made.

My continuous insistence, amounting at times very near to threat—no *pesantren,* no money—that I visit some of these schools finally led, toward the end of my stay, to my being allowed to go off to the interior for a day to do so with a young, very pious theology student I had run into in the marketplace. I got to three. One had a government school formally attached to it. ("We go to school so we won't be deceived," one boy said to me; "we study in the *pesantren* so we won't deceive.") The second was rudimentary, a few peasants hanging around a mosque. But the third was the real thing: two hundred students, ranging in age from twelve to forty-seven, drawn from all over Aceh; a graded and developed curriculum reaching into the higher levels of religious scholarship—*fiqh, tafsīr, uṣūl, taṣawwuf;* full-time, intensive study; a large and beautiful, Acehnese pavilion-style mosque; and a teacher famous (like his grandfather and great-grandfather before him) as both a textual scholar and a sufi adept, who was also a leader of a movement formed to resist the intrusion of Western ideas of education, or indeed of anything else, into the fixed and sufficient *pesantren* world.

Despite the closed, inward-looking air of this school, I was received not with distrust but with warmth. In part this was owing to the presence of my escort, who had studied there for a while, and of whom great things were now expected as an Islamic intellectual. But mostly it was because a famous American professor, as my escort assured them I was, had recognized that this was indeed the place to come if one wanted to see "real" Islam. Indeed, the students almost immediately set about to arrange a great debate between the American visitor and the teacher-director of the place, also most affable toward me, so as to pit "Western" against "Muslim" science.

We gathered in the mosque, a circle of packed-together students with the teacher—the word is *ustād,* "master," "professor," so let us call him that—and me standing in a cleared space at the center.

I began by explaining why I had come there. There were some general questions, mostly about the relation of Muslims to the government in the United States, and then the debate began. The *ustād* asked me whether I believed that the American astronauts had in fact landed on the moon. (This was the second anniversary of the landing, and the Acehnese papers were full of nervous discussions of it.) I said, yes, I did, but that I understood that many Acehnese did not, which drew a large laugh. The *ustād* said that no Muslim could believe it because of a tradition from the Prophet, that is, a hadith, concerning Noah's flood. The Prophet is held to have said that an enormous ocean lies between the earth and the moon and this was the source of the flood. If the Americans had gone to the moon they would have put a hole in this ocean and a flood like Noah's, drowning us all, would have ensued.

I didn't quite know what to say to this and confined myself to describing, as best I could, what Western science considered the moon to be, its origins, why it shines, and so on. Not the strongest of replies, but I felt I had better not, not just then, not just there, question the authority of a hadith. My escort, who later told me that, like most educated Muslims, in Aceh or anywhere else, he himself believed that Americans had indeed gone to the moon, said, jokingly, almost mockingly, perhaps they went around the edge of the ocean.

The *ustād* was unmoved, and unannoyed, by any of this. He said, still mildly (he sounded both like a man sincerely trying to find out and like one who already knew, as I suppose I did myself), that the astronauts could not have gone to the moon because the one thing that is impossible is that the Prophet could be wrong. What he thought had actually happened was analogous to what happened to Nimrod in the Quran. Nimrod was an atheist. He went up in the sky to kill God. (Getting into the spirit of things, I said, he didn't believe there was a God and yet he went off to kill him?—and got an appreciative laugh from the students, who were enjoying this immensely.) Nimrod shot his gun (actually his arrow, but that's a detail), God caught the bullet, smeared it with blood, and threw it back to him. Nimrod then went back to the earth and said, see, I have killed God, he is just another mortal. But in fact he had been only the victim of God's infinite power and, I suppose, sense of humor. That was how it was with the astronauts. They *thought,* in all good faith, that they were on the moon, but they really weren't. God, not wanting to disappoint them after all the effort they had put in, had constructed a fake moon off to the side somewhere for them to land on.

I didn't really know what to do with this argument either, so I just said that maybe the best thing would be for a Muslim to go along on the trip next time, and we disbanded. I had had my journey to the heart of the heart of the country. West met East, Reason engaged Faith, Modernity confronted Tradition . . . story jostled story: a clash of narratives. Nothing was disturbed. Nothing you could see.

The last time I saw Fez, a quarter-century after the first time I saw it—in both instances as a labyrinth of papers and permissions bureaucrats impeding my progress to Sefrou—it seemed to be finally, definitively, losing its looks. Of course, it had been losing them and then more or less putting them back together again for centuries. "Fez is . . . the oldest city in Morocco," to quote once more the distant, superior, but marvelously observant Edith Wharton, who saw it for a few days in 1917, ". . . yet it would be truer to say of it, as of all Moroccan cities, that it has no age, since its seemingly immutable shape is for ever crumbling and becoming renewed on the old lines . . . The passion for building seems allied, in this country of inconsequences, to the supine indifference that lets existing constructions crumble back to clay." The trouble, or perhaps it was an advance, was that this time it was not being reassembled. It was being reimagined.

A motor road was built in the late seventies, designed to make it possible for tourists, so many of them elderly, so many of them nervous, to avoid the hour or two of walking, down hill and up (for Fez is shaped a bit like a soup bowl), through narrow, cobbled

streets, crowded with people, goods, debris, and animals, necessary to get to the famous mosques and markets at the heart of the old city. But local opposition and, so it is said, administrative corruption impressive even for Fez caused it not to extend across the whole city as originally planned, but stopped it midway. Tour buses, taxis, trucks, motorcycles, and various other sorts of vehicles pour down into the center at the bottom of the bowl and then have to turn about and struggle up out again the way they have come, creating a continuous stream of angry traffic—a great scar, as the inhabitants put it, on the belly of the city. The abandonment of the old city by its rich and middle-class inhabitants, and even, finally, by many of its working-class ones, for sprawling, centerless neighborhoods growing up around and about it has reached massive proportions. This is general now in Morocco, with the collapse of classic urbanity we have already seen for Sefrou. But Fez being Fez, not only "the oldest city in Morocco" but the most jealous and self-regarding, the changes seem, to those who see themselves as the children of its unmatchable civilization, to be especially grave: a decline into ordinariness.

There are other outrages. Along the northeast edge of the old city there are haphazard new sections, built by rural in-migrants with remittances from relatives working abroad, which the city government has sought to make at least look Fez-like by prescribing appropriate facades. Off to the south there are, clustered around a new palace the king has had built to house distinguished foreign guests, *nouveau riche* neighborhoods with massy and multicolored homes that have grown so presumptuous (the locals call one tract "Al-Dallas," after the American soap opera, another "Al-Farouk," after the Egyptian voluptuary) that the king has issued edicts, not much observed since most of the owners are clients of his, against constructing any more of them. Off to the east, in the middle of a bare plain, there is a great white Saudi palace, complete with landing field and, so I was assured, walled-off harem, built by King Fahd as a place to stay when he is in town. A fine old pasha's house, since the Protectorate a quiet and graceful garden hotel, appropriately worn, has been turned into a plush, couscous-and-kaftans tourist trap. An even grander hotel, modern in the American manner, has been built by the government on the town's most spectacular viewing site, amid the ruined tombs of its most famous dynasty. (This last, for the moment, is a ruin itself. It was burned to the ground in the labor riots of 1990.)

There is much more for the nostalgic to deplore (a charmless university carved out of a nondescript army camp, once-wooded hillsides covered with anonymous housing developments, impoverished squatters camping in the fountained gardens and mosaic apartments of the abandoned grand family houses of the old city), and the nostalgic seem never to tire of deploring it. But there are a number of places where, at least for a moment and to an extent, the reimagined city can be mentally pushed aside and the prospects of a reassembled one thought to be, perhaps, not wholly beyond effective reach. Some of these are, of course, deeply traditional—the grand mosques, a couple of the brotherhoods, one or two of the craft bazaars. Others, however, are products of a more immediate past: the Fez that colonialism made and nationalism, as culturally conservative here as it was politically radical, took over. For example, there is the Collège Moulay Idris, where, late in 1985, the Japanese ambassador to Morocco gave a speech to the *anciens élèves* at their annual reunion on the necessity of preserving the heritage, character, and equilibrium of Fez.

The Collège Moulay Idris (Moulay Idris, a descendant of the Prophet immigrant from Arabia after the Shia wars, is the purported founder of Fez in 789) was one of those institutions found in a number of colonial territories—Achimota in the Gold Coast, the Presidency Colleges in Calcutta, Madras, and Bombay—an elite academy set up to form a select, cultivated, school-loyal (and, of course, all male) cadre of western-educated "natives" who could mediate between, in this case, the higher reaches of French and Muslim civilization. And, as with most such enterprises, it was not unsuccessful, though, as with most, the mediation turned out to be of a rather different sort than those who designed it had in mind. The Collège became, as one writer has called it, "the Eton of the Moroccan political elite": a forcing ground for turning a hundred or two of the children of traditional Fez notables into ardent nationalists. Today it not only continues, somewhat Arabized, a little bit democratized, as a cultural stronghold for the socially advantaged, but its old-boy alumni remain a cohesive and powerful group within the city: "Fassi squared," as they like to put it.

The Collège, which is located at the gate to the one "bourgeois" residential quarter of the old city still somewhat functioning as such, is a graceful, "neo-Moorish" building with an inlaid ceiling, carved wooden interiors, an enclosed garden, tiled fountains, covered walkways, a rare book library, and an air-conditioned auditorium. The ambassador's address was an invitation-only occasion (I was there, by grace of the chairman of the alumni association, the rector of the Faculty of Literature at the University of Fez), a *tout Fès* ingathering of perhaps four hundred people.

The Japanese ambassador, who spoke in impeccable French after being introduced by the rector in literary Arabic, talked of the difficulty and the necessity of maintaining traditional cultural equilibrium. Japan had undergone enormous changes over the course of its history. But, through it all, it had conserved the sources of its personality. The Chinese influence on Japan, the Kyoto efflorescence, the Tokugawa synthesis, the intrusion of the West, the Meiji restoration, the triumph of the militarists, and the economic dynamism of the past forty years all demonstrate the virtue, through good times and terrible, of keeping a balance between the forces of change and the pull of tradition.

There are, in fact, he said, very strong parallels between Fez and Kyoto. Both combine monarchic loyalty with popular democracy. Both are intensely traditional and subject to strong Western influence. Both have significantly altered their mode of life while keeping their spirit intact. Both are the cradles of their nation's civilization. Even during the Second World War American scholars kept Kyoto from being bombed, showing that people, such as themselves, who appreciate the value of art and religion, history and learning, who care for continuity and ancient things, can have a positive, humane effect, under even the most difficult of conditions. The recovery of Japan after the disaster that the militarist adventure produced, a recovery from ground zero, is proof that neither blind traditionalism nor headlong modernism can in itself bring about a healthy society and a great civilization. There must, he concluded, be an equilibrium between them, an equilibrium such as that the students and alumni of Moulay Idris were seeking, also under the most difficult of conditions, to maintain in Fez, the Moroccan Kyoto.

Japanese culturalism and Moroccan, the moral interplay of Asia, America, Europe, and the Maghreb, the reassembled past and the reimagined, crumbling grandeur and unbombed history: the tumble of images was dizzying, irony upon irony. One, not the least reverberant, perhaps only the ambassador and I were in a position to catch. (He remarked on it himself when we chatted for a while during the reception beforehand.) His address was delivered, it just so happened, on Pearl Harbor day.

ↄ

What do such anecdotal portraits of the ethnographer as a young . . . middle-aged . . . aging . . . man demonstrate? Not that much about either him or the people he "studied." Different tales, easily producible from four thousand pages of hurried fieldnotes and vast stockpiles of scattered memory, could be as carefully arranged as these have been to produce quite different impressions. What they demonstrate is that to be an American anthropologist during the second half of the twentieth century in the "Third World" (the term itself, by now, a period piece) is to know what it is to be a sign of the times.

The headline events of current history, the ones that mark out the present direction of things, rarely appear in anthropological accounts, which concern themselves with what they take to be profounder and more lasting matters. But, especially now that the world has become so thoroughly interconnected, it is increasingly difficult to keep them at bay. And if in addition one comes from a country seen to be near the center of those events and implicated in them—Suez, Vietnam, the Bay of Pigs, the death of Lumumba, the Six-Day War—one is not only not free of them but, willy-nilly, some sort of stand-in for them. There are lots of advantages in being the citizen of a superpower in less prominent places, but cultural invisibility is not among them.

Working in first Indonesia, then Morocco, and then both, from 1952, when Eisenhower announced "I shall go to Korea" and Farouk fled Egypt, to 1986, when the *Challenger* exploded and Chernoble burned, there was never a time when "the West" in general, and the United States in particular, did not intrude in one way or another upon my daily encounters, to say nothing of my state of mind. The comparison I have been tracing between Indonesia and Morocco as independent entities alternately engaged by a generalized visitor happening by is rather more complicated than I have represented it to be. There is a third term, so far suppressed: the larger world which propelled me toward them.

And them toward me: from the onset of Independence—Indonesia in 1950, Morocco in 1956—both countries were engaged in a determined struggle to join that larger world. For all the worrying attention paid to the rearrangements of global power relations, trade flows, and cultural affiliations that the decolonization of Asia and Africa set in motion between the late forties and the early eighties, their full import has not as yet been sufficiently appreciated. If anything anymore really counts as a revolution, rather than a mere reshuffling of persons and positions, this does. It not only remade the absolute map, it changed the sense of what it mapped—what a country is. In 1950 there were fifty-eight members of the United Nations, most of them Western. In 1980 there were a hundred and fifty-eight, most of them not.

It was in this interval, between the age of Ho, Nehru, Nkrumah, Mossadegh, and Sukarno and that of Mobutu, Marcos, Indira Gandhi, Khomeini, and Sadat, that Indonesia and Morocco, the first rather emphatically, the second more warily, entered in their own names as actors upon the international scene, a circumstance that gave their citizens, even the most passive and out of touch of them, a particular sense of what went on there, and what was at stake. World events looked different to someone whose country was trying to reinforce its place within them from the way they looked to people whose country was trying to find it.

For a country trying to find its place, the issues it faced were almost entirely regional, or even subregional; but the context in which it engaged them was through-and-through global. Great-power tensions, great-power maneuvers, and great-power crises invaded just about everything, enveloping parochial conflicts in larger concerns, without making them any less parochial. The Korean war, the Japanese resurgence, and the Vietnam war on the one hand, the Algerian war, the Islamic resurgence, and the Arab-Israeli conflict on the other, constructed the environment within which the specific pursuits of national interest—Indonesia's acquisition of Western New Guinea in 1963 or its seizure of Eastern Timor in 1975, Morocco's border clashes with Algeria in 1963 or its march into the Sahara in 1971—were carried out.

The regional quality of the two countries' involvement in "foreign affairs" that sets them in quite different sorts of political neighborhoods, as well as the global context which connects those neighborhoods, is perhaps most effectively evoked by a mere tabulation of some of the world-news events that occurred in and around Indonesia in East and Southeast Asia and in and around Morocco in North Africa and the Middle East during the fifties, sixties, and seventies (see accompanying table).

There are a number of matters less easily encapsulated in such a table, because they are pervading realities rather than particular events—the headlong ascent of Japan and swarming labor migration to recovering Europe, the dangerous magic of oil and the ambiguous effects of the green revolution. And in both cases, there is, or anyway was, the most pervasive reality of all: the Cold War. But the merest glance at the two chronologies, as schematic as they

Chronology of Events: 1950–1979

Date	East and Southeast Asia	Middle East and North Africa
1950–53	Korean War	
1954	Dienbienphu; SEATO formed	
1954–62		Algerian War and independence
1955	Bandung Conference	
1956		Suez Crisis; Tunisia independent
1957	Malaya independent	
1958	Regional rebellion in Sumatra and the Celebes	Oil found in Libya
1960		Mauritania independent
1961	Open U.S. involvement in Vietnam begins	
1961–62	West New Guinea (Irian) crisis	
1963	Federation of Malaysia formed	
1963–66	"Confrontation" with Malaysia	
1963–70		Morocco-Algeria border clashes
1964	Tonkin Gulf resolution; China explodes A-bomb	Americans evacuate former French bases in Morocco held since 1950
1965–66	Failed coup, massacres, change of regime	Ben Barka affair
1966	Cultural revolution begins in China	
1967	Association of Southeast Asian Nations (ASEAN) formed	Six-Day War
1969		Qaddafi overthrows Idris I in Libya
1971	Vietnam war ends	First failed coup (Skhirat)
1972	Nixon in China; Marcos declares martial law in Philippines	Second failed coup (Kenitra)
1973		Formation of Polisario; Yom Kippur/Ramadan War
1975	Indonesian invasion of East Timor	

Chronology of Events: 1950–1979 *(continued)*

Date	East and Southeast Asia	Middle East and North Africa
1976	Mao, Chou die; Khmer Rouge killings begin in Cambodia	Spanish cede Western Sahara to Morocco and Mauritania; Saharan War begins
1977	SEATO dissolved; Deng begins reforms in China	
1979	Vietnamese regime displaces Khmer Rouge in Cambodia	Shah falls in Iran, Khomeini to power; Mauritania withdraws from Saharan War

are, demonstrates that though part (a marginal part in most cases) of the worldwide scuffle of contending powers, the two countries are located in that scuffle at quite distinctive points. As much as their towns, their languages, their politics, and their religious styles, their international involvements are palpably different.

Morocco, both in the Arab world and at the African edge of it (a member at once of the Arab League and the Organization of African Unity), as well as culturally connected to France and Spain, found itself subject to radically different claims upon its loyalties. It sent troops to the Arab-Israeli wars in 1967 and 1973, though they managed to arrive too late to be actively deployed, and, in the early sixties, to the U.N. force set up to bring the Congo-Zaire civil war under control. It quarreled to the point of armed conflict with its most immediate neighbor, Algeria, whose long struggle for independence it had strongly supported, over the ill-drawn boundary between them. Its domestic politics spilled over into France, with the conspiratorial murder in Paris, by French policemen and Moroccan soldiers, of the leading politician opposed to the throne. And with the withdrawal by Spain, following the death of Franco, from the Western Sahara, it proclaimed the territory its own and became involved in a full-scale war with nationalist Saharans that at once isolated it from virtually all its neighbors and drove it to greater and greater dependence upon the West and the oil-rich kingdoms of the Middle East. By the 1980s, embattled and improvisatory, it had become a three-way client state: to Mitterand's France, Fahd's Saudi Arabia, and Reagan's United States.

Indonesia, at the crossroads between continental Asia, Australia, and the Western Pacific, in a region as culturally motley as it is ethnically miscellaneous, found itself less torn by the claims of neighbors upon its national loyalties than beset by virtually every major ideological force at play in the world: Communism, Soviet and Chinese; Islamism, radical and accommodative; Third World nationalism; Japanese neo-mercantilism. Like Morocco it had but little time to sort matters out. And, like Morocco, it was unable to avoid violence in doing so.

Led, until 1965, by one of the gaudier heroes of the heroic phase of the Third World revolution, the romantical and clamorous Sukarno, Indonesia had a far more turbulent entry into international politics than Morocco under the quieter, more calculating Hassan II. By 1955, five years after the transfer of sovereignty, Sukarno was already reaching for Third World leadership in convening the first Afro-Asian Conference in Bandung: representatives of twenty-nine countries—Chou and Nehru, Nasser and U Nu, Sihanouk and Muhammed Ali. Nor was the rest of his regime any less excited. There was the campaign to annex Western New Guinea. (The takeover of Dutch enterprises, the threats and feints of military action, the final success via the mediating activities of Robert Kennedy and Ellsworth Bunker.) There was the opposition to the formation of Malaysia, "British colonialism in a new form"—the threat to "crush" it, the withdrawal from the U.N. when it was seated on the Security Council, the sacking of the British embassy in Jakarta. And there were "Guided Democracy," the rise of the Indonesian Communist Party to near dominance, and the popular convulsion that destroyed them both.

After Suharto displaced Sukarno in 1966, the theatrics were muffled. The Malaysian confrontation was ended, Indonesia returned to the U.N., the Communist leaders who had not perished in the massacres or gone into exile were imprisoned or executed, the sedate Association of Southeast Asian States replaced the rambunctious Afro-Asiatic movement as the vehicle of regional diplomacy, friendly relations with Holland were restored, foreign aid and investment began to flow again. But in 1975 matters grew tense once more. The withdrawal of Portugal, after the coup in Lisbon, from its mini-colony in the eastern half of the island of Timor led to an outbreak of local nationalism there. The Indonesian army thereupon invaded to put it down. Widespread international protest, especially from the Third World and Iron Curtain countries, and a U.N. resolution demanding withdrawal followed. With American, Japanese, and Western European support, the storm was weathered, and by 1980 the country, though still maintaining a formal neutrality in the Cold War, was about as clearly tilted toward the West as, under Sukarno, it had been toward the East.

It is unnecessary to go any further into the details of all this to make the point I want to make. Field research in such times, in such places, is not a matter of working free from the cultural baggage you have brought with you so as to enter, without shape and without attachment, into a foreign mode of life. It is a matter of living out your existence in two stories at once.

One of these stories is the familiar one of the anthropologist projecting him- or herself onto the local scene as a minor actor, odd but harmless, and a solemn observer, searching out assorted facts. The other is the less familiar one, rarely recounted, of his or her attempt to maintain such a reduced and specialized persona amid the currents and cross-currents of world-scale politics—the struggle for hegemonies, broad or narrow, persistent or fleeting. The refractions of that struggle, as my little stories are meant to illustrate, are virtually everywhere in countries as assertive and consequential, and at times ambitious, as Indonesia and Morocco. Sputniks, foreign bases, diplomatic adventures, international con-

ferences, aid missions, and cultural exchanges are not external to
what the anthropologist finds before him, in Bali or Aceh, Marrakech or the Middle Atlas; they are ingredient in it. You may set
out to isolate yourself from cosmopolitan concerns and contain
your interests within hermetical contexts. But the concerns follow
you. The contexts explode.

5

Disciplines

My dictionary, not the most capacious but extensive enough, lists seven definitions for the noun "discipline": (1) Training that is expected to produce a specified character or pattern of behavior, especially that which is expected to produce moral or mental improvement. (2) Controlled behavior resulting from such training. (3) A systematic method to obtain obedience: a *military discipline.* (4) A state of order based upon submission to rules and authority. (5) Punishment intended to correct or train. (6) A set of rules or methods, [such] as those regulating a church or monastic order. (7) A branch of knowledge or teaching. In addition there are two verbal meanings ("to train by instruction and control; teach to obey rules or accept authority" and "to punish or penalize"), as well as a recommendation to "see synonyms at *teach, punish.*" The OED has twenty-one (fifteen nounal, six verbal) and the usual string of citations, the most reverberant perhaps being one from *Troilus and Cressida:* "Heauen blesse thee from a Tutor and Discipline come not neere thee."

The idea of a discipline, in any of these senses on whose ironies and cross-actions Michel Foucault built so much of his rhetorical tower, fits anthropology none too well. At once broad and general, wildly aspiring ("The Study of Man"), and particular and miscellaneous, strangely obsessive (puberty rites, gift exchange, kin terminology), it has always had, both to itself and to outsiders, a blurry image. Neither method nor subject matter very exactly defines it. ("Ethnography" has been often proposed with respect to the first, "primitive society" with respect to the second. But the one is as diffuse an idea as that it is supposed to clarify and the other is misconceived.) What theory it has had, not all that much, has been borrowed from elsewhere—Marx, Freud, Saussure, or Darwin. Nor does the notion of "a scholarly tradition" help much: the sorts of study prosecuted in its name, comparative mythography to ethnobotany, are impossibly diverse.

Anthropology, or anyway social or cultural anthropology, is in fact rather more something one picks up as one goes along year after year trying to figure out what it is and how to practice it than something one has instilled in one through "a systematic method to obtain obedience" or formalized "train[ing] by instruction and control." It is, of course, taught, sometimes fiercely with lots of rules to obey and authority to respect, and it has it own ways, from book reviews to tenure decisions, of inflicting "punishment intended to correct." But the "specified character or pattern of behavior," to say nothing of the "moral or mental improvement," does not very reliably emerge. The blurred image is earned: there is indeed a lack of firm edge and defined target to what we do, however hard some may work to disguise the fact. Perhaps this is a scandal, perhaps it is a strength. But in either case it makes any attempt to characterize the field synoptically something of an exercise in special pleading.

This does not prevent such attempts from continually being made—the very diffuseness of things encourages them. Of all the human sciences, anthropology is perhaps the most given to questioning itself as to what it is and coming up with answers that sound more like overall world views or declarations of faith than they do like descriptions of "a branch of knowledge." With the changes in scholarly life in recent years that have scrambled together much that was formerly reasonably well separated—history, philosophy, science, the arts—the difficulty of giving a straightforward, matter-of-fact account of what, if you say you are an anthropologist, you ought to be doing has only increased. The first index entry nowadays in books surveying the field is often: "anthropology, crisis of . . ."

Yet the "crisis" may be an optical illusion—the result of trying to define "anthropology" as one would define "English," or "linguistics," or "entomology," as the study of something or other, rather than as a loose collection of intellectual careers. Inside this indisciplined discipline there may be but so many vocations trying to define themselves. In my case, anyway, that is the case. It is in the trajectory of my professional life, neither regular nor representative, very fitfully planned, very inspecifically aimed, that the anthropologist is to be found. Here, too, the matter is *ad hoc* and *ex post*. You see what you have been doing (if you see it at all) after you have been doing it.

The question is the more difficult because over time "anthropology," however conceived, is a far from stable enterprise. What it was in 1950, when, stumbling out of an undergraduate major in English and philosophy and looking for something rather more connected to the world as it was, I first wandered into it; in 1960, when, properly licensed, I first began to contribute to "the literature"; in 1970, when, a professor in an institution commonly referred to as illustrious, I found those contributions starting to be discussed and evaluated; in 1980, when, cited all over the place, they were dissected, resisted, corrected, distorted, celebrated, decried, or built upon—these are hardly the same thing. Other fields change as well of course, some of them more rapidly or fundamentally; but few do so in so hard to locate a way as anthropology. It alters like a mood, an attitude, or a climate of opinion.

In trying to say, nonetheless, what anthropology "is"—not from an all-over, bird's eye view, a stratagem that may be left to textbooks, which play a minor role in either the formation or the consolidation of anthropological thought, but from the perspective of the progress of one of its more determined pilgrims (but determined upon what?) making his way through its promises and discouragements—two approaches seem workable: (1) an account of the shifts in intellectual outlook in the discipline, as one found oneself caught up in them; (2) a similar description of similar shifts in the conditions of work, what some would call, but (again) I will not, the modes of anthropological production. As the two are intricately linked (though not in the way the modes-of-production conception imagines) they must, however, be discussed together. Theory and practice are not, as idealists suppose, cause and outcome. Nor are they, as materialists do, outcome and cause. They are pursuits in a calling.

ᠭᠣ

The Harvard Social Relations Department in 1950 was nothing if not characteristic of its time: a period, contrary to its reputation, of a great deal of intellectual ferment and innovation, and above all, so far as the social sciences were concerned, of a sense that things were at last coming firmly together. "The Sociology is About to Begin said the Man with the Loudspeaker," Talcott Parsons, in his presidential address to the American Sociological Association no less, reported his two young children marching importantly about the house proclaiming. And indeed for a while it really seemed so.

For the most part, the feeling that a new era was dawning was a reflex of an end-of-the-war reanimation much more powerful than, after a half-century of receding horizons, is now remembered. The subsidized students of the G.I. Bill generation (of which I was one), older, less unformed, more anxious to put diversion aside and get on with things than undergraduates had typically been, began to arrive at the graduate schools, infusing them with a new seriousness. The professoriate, many of whose members had spent the war in some sort of planning, intelligence, or propaganda work, was exhilarated by the prospect of pursuing its own agendas again, armed with the real-world experience it had gained serving the nation. The emergence of the United States as a world power, indeed *the* world power, reviving Europe, containing the Soviet Union, setting the Third World on its developmental course, seemed to suggest that the headquarters of learning and research had moved here as well. And of course we were rich then; richer than anybody else by far. If you could think of anything at all plausible to do, you could get the money someplace—from the National Science Foundation, the Office of Naval Research, or the National Institutes of Mental Health, from Ford or Rockefeller or Rand or the Social Science Research Council—to do it.

The Social Relations Department had been formed, not without opposition, in 1946 by a handful of nationally prominent professors, mostly in their forties, dissatisfied with their own fields as then defined and anxious to rearrange things so as to produce a more broadly integrative approach in the social sciences. There were four subfields, sociology, social psychology, clinical psychology, and social anthropology. Students were admitted into one of these subfields and expected to pursue careers within it, but they were obligated to take courses and pass examinations in each of the others as well. Driven forward by a resounding call to arms the insurgents had put together, "Toward a Common Language for the Areas of the Social Sciences" (why not English?, some unreconstructed wit inquired), it was nothing if not interdisciplinary. It lasted twenty-five years, only about fifteen of them genuinely innovative. After that things went, as they normally do, back to normal.

It was, in any case, social science in full cry; headier and more confident than before or since. There was the project for a grandly architectonic "general theory of social action" that Parsons, the chairman of the department and its presiding spirit, had put in motion—a great assemblage of boxes and arrows that he sometimes spoke of as the sociological equivalent of the Newtonian system, sometimes as an effort to split the social atom. There was the Psychological Clinic, under the somewhat Jungian, somewhat Freudian, altogether eclectic Henry Murray, dedicated to systematizing and testing psychoanalytical insights in a properly scientific manner. There was the Russian Research Center, directed by the anthropologist Clyde Kluckhohn, employing social scientific techniques (refugee interviewing, content analysis) in an effort to penetrate, and foil, Soviet intentions. There was the Laboratory of Social Relations, led by the methodologist Samuel Stouffer, perfecting statistical measures and survey techniques. There was the Ramah Project, also under Kluckhohn, engaged in a long-term comparative study of values in five adjacent cultures in the American Southwest. A group around the social psychologist Jerome Bruner was just beginning to develop what eventually turned out to be cognitive psychology, another around the sociologist George Homans was working on small-group studies, another around the aging polymath Pitirim Sorokin was trying to put his sweeping and rather theatrical ideas on historical evolution into more researchable form.

For someone whose previous acquaintance with the social sciences had been limited to some courses in fiscal policy, an undergraduate thesis trying to marry Freud to Spinoza, and a literary exposure to Ruth Benedict's *Patterns of Culture,* it was all a bit much. Finding one's way through this maze of grand possibilities, only loosely related, and some even in fairly serious tension with one another, was, however exciting (and it was enormously exciting), a perilous business. With so many ways to turn, so few tracks laid down, and so little experience of one's own to go by, even small decisions, to take this seminar, attack that subject, work with this professor, seemed enormously consequential—a reverseless commitment to something immense, portentous, splendid, and unclear.

In this maze or maelstrom, or vanity fair, the anthropologist had one thing going for him in keeping himself reasonably on course: the realization, immediately instilled in him (or—there were a few women—in her) and continuously reinforced, that he was going to have to do fieldwork. Unlike the others, mere academicians, we had a testing ahead, a place we had to go to and a rite we had to go through. The prospect of this moment of truth (though in my case it turned out to be two and a half years) wonderfully concentrated our minds, gave us a powerful sense of moving toward something, or anyway somewhere. The problem was where, and it filled our consciousness—at least it filled mine—almost all the time. Where was our Trobriands, our Nuerland, our Tepoztlan to be? A much more important question, actually, than what we would do (one could always think of something, so much was unstudied) when we got there.

But here too the progress was more accidental than purposive. The very day I arrived in Cambridge a professor, trying to be kind but failing, asked me where I was going to work. As I was barely aware at that point that this was a consideration I said, dissembling madly, well maybe Latin America. Fortunately, he did not pursue the matter, which would have been uncomfortable for both of us. But I did, as a result, spend the next year or so thinking vaguely of Brazil, which I understood to have some Indians in it, and giving that as an answer whenever the question came up, as it did with great regularity, particularly among students.

In the summer after my first year, Kluckhohn gave me a research job on the five cultures project, studying differential reactions of the cultures (one talked in those days of cultures as agents) to what were taken to be problems common to them all—drought, death, and alcoholism. (I did not actually go to the Southwest but merely worked from reports and fieldnotes stored in Cambridge.) This raised a more concrete possibility, but one about which I was quite wary because of the industrial social science aspects of it all: dozens of researchers, from all sorts of fields, working in a grand variety of ways on a grand variety of topics, all of it rather too closely managed from corporate headquarters at Harvard. Those days anyway, the ideal of alone among the unknown, what has been called the "my people" syndrome, was still very much alive, and there were depreciative murmurs to be heard about "gas station anthropology" and "meadow work rather than fieldwork." In any case, the question became moot when at the end of the summer yet another professor walked into the office in the Peabody Museum where I was blithely sorting Navajo ways of mourning from Zuni and both from Mormon, Texan, and Spanish American, never having myself so much as been to a funeral. He said (he was a man of few words, mostly abrupt): "We are forming a team to go to Indonesia. We need someone on religion and someone on kinship. Do you and your wife want to go?" I said, hardly knowing more than where Indonesia was, and that inexactly, "Yes, we would." I went home to tell my wife what had happened, and we set out to discover what I had gotten us into.

What I had gotten us into was the very stamp and image of the Social Relations Idea: a well-financed, multidisciplinary, long-term, team field project directed toward the study not of an isolated tribal culture but of a two-thousand-year-old civilization fully in the throes of revolutionary change. Of the nine members of the team, six, a sociologist, three anthropologists, a social psychologist, and a clinical psychologist, were from the Social Relations Department as such; of the other three, two were anthropologists from the established Anthropology Department, from which the Social Relations program was in some sense a breakaway, and one was an historian of China, seconded in from Far Eastern Studies. The collective aim of the group, though it was generally assumed that it was supposed to have one, was unclear. So was how it was, on the ground, going to operate, how it was to be organized, what it was going to focus upon. We were to go to Java, descend upon a location apparently already chosen, and, paired with Javanese counterparts from Gadjah Mada, the revolutionary university set up only a few years earlier in Jogjakarta, study assorted aspects of "the culture"—family, religion, village life, social stratification, the market, the Chinese. Then, talking to one another all the while, and perhaps even sharing fieldnotes (though that never occurred), we were to return and write doctoral theses.

But if there were no aims, or at least no readily stateable ones, there were assumptions. There was the idea that the time had come for anthropology to turn away from its nearly exclusive focus on "primitives" and begin to investigate large-scale societies directly in the stream of contemporary history. There was the idea that it should also turn away from intellectual isolation, cultural particularism, mindless empiricism, and the lone ranger approach to research and begin to work together with other, more conceptualized disciplines (psychology, economics, sociology, political science) in a big-push effort to construct a unified, generalizing science of society from which could emerge a practical technology for the management of human affairs. And there was the idea that the groundwork for such a science had already been laid by the great social theorists of the "long nineteenth century," the one that ended with the First World War—Marx, Freud, Weber, Pareto, Simmel, Durkheim, somewhat latterly, Malinowski. All that was needed was systematization, funding, and the perfection of method. With that, and resolution, we would have, reasonably soon, something worth being compared if not to physics at least to physiology.

That, of course, never happened, has still not happened, and, in my opinion anyway, is no nearer to happening now than it was then. The project as it unfolded undermined in its very success (for it was, again in my opinion, and by my standards, quite successful) any expectation that "science" here could mean what it apparently meant for Harvey or Pasteur—the depiction of machinery and the concoction of remedies. What it might mean instead, what other conceptions of knowledge, of knowing, and of the uses of knowledge could be brought into play, was, however, obscure. Making it a bit less obscure became, in the actual course of my work, under the actual conditions in which I pursued it, my governing purpose; and it has remained so since.

After a year of collective, speaking-and-hearing study of the Indonesian language, which had the side effect of allowing us to get to know one another well enough to decide not to try to coordinate our individual research activities into the sort of unified enterprise the project's designers had in mind but to be a "team" in only the loosest and most collegiate sense, we set off via Rotterdam for the three-week sea voyage to Jakarta. When we got to Jogjakarta, another day's train ride inland, to meet our Indonesian collaborators, we had something of a surprise waiting for us: they were dubious indeed about both us and the project—skeptical of our capacities, opposed to our plans, suspicious of our intentions.

The immediate problem was that the director of the project, the professor who had so laconically invited me into it, had announced on the very eve of our departure that he would not be accompanying us; he was withdrawing from the enterprise for reasons of health. He had traveled to Jogjakarta the year before to make the arrangements for the research with the three senior professors—a customary law scholar, an agricultural economist, and a linguist—who had been appointed to be his co-directors on the Indonesian side, but he had told us virtually nothing of what had transpired. We therefore arrived not only leaderless, without the established figure with whom the professors had dealt and whom they had apparently trusted, but as a motley band of obscure and inexperienced graduate students, who had, moreover, the presumptuousness to find the arrangements that had supposedly been agreed to not to their liking.

Indeed, we found them unworkable. The plan was that we would go up to a mountainous area north of Jogjakarta where there was an old Dutch resort hotel, now unoccupied. We would live there, in comfort and safety, together with the, it now turned out, not five or six but something like fifteen or twenty, twenty or thirty (it never became very clear) Indonesian students whom the professors would select. Under the general surveillance of the professors, who were apparently going to commute from Jogjakarta on the weekends, we would summon people in from the countryside round and about—or, more exactly, local officials, who would know who was appropriate, would summon them for us. Working from a prepared schedule of topics, we would interview these people in groups (so they could correct one another, and come to a consensual view) about this or that matter. Then we would prepare a report of our findings and depart. This was how Dutch scholars of *Volkenkunde* and their native assistants now become our mentors had worked. Standing where, perhaps twenty years earlier, those mentors had stood, subaltern apprentices there to be useful, we too, therefore, would work that way.

It would be hard to conceive an image of social research more entirely opposed to our notions, and those of our own mentors, the people who had sent us to Java in the first place, than this extraordinary reincarnation of the pith-helmet procedures of colonial ethnology. We were caught between academic mentalities, one ambitious, confident, and ultramodern, one nostalgic, defensive, and obsolescent; stranded between paradigms in an epistemic break that, this being Indonesia in 1951 and we being Americans, was a moral and political break as well. Making our way across that break, which, at length, with difficulty, and at the cost of injured feelings all around, we managed to do, was an instructive experience: an introduction to "the field" that made it clear that, like theories, methods, projects, and researchers, research sites are not found, they are made, and it is these things that make them.

What separated the Indonesians and ourselves was less where to go (though one of the few parts of central Java where it was too cold to grow much rice, where an armed gang of leftist rebels controlled much of the countryside, and which was dominated by a famous relic of late colonialism, didn't entirely attract), but what the "going" was going to consist in. Given their determination not to be subordinates any longer in their own country, their wish to bring their students up to speed, their hierarchical conception of scholarship, their questions about our real intentions (we were never able to convince them that we were not government sponsored), and, not least, their desire that we get in and out of the country without untoward incident, indeed without anyone much even knowing we had been there, the Indonesians naturally wanted a maximally controlled situation—an anthropological white room. Given our view of ourselves as paladins of an improved, "cutting edge" social science, our assumption that our work would benefit not just ourselves but our subjects, our doubts about the qualifications (and the real function) of the Indonesian students so peremptorily assigned to us, and, not least, our conviction that what we wanted to do demanded free, intimate, and long-term relations with those we were studying, isolated from external oversight and the attentions of the state, we naturally wanted a maximally uncontrolled situation—the Trobriands in Java.

Looking back at this intercultural drama, the willful West meets the put-upon East, what is striking is how vividly it reflects, in its unselfconscious, almost parodical way, what has widely come to be seen in the decades since to be the moral crux of ethnographical inquiry. This crux has been set forth in varying ways, with varying degrees of angst and self-righteousness: What gives *us* the right to study *them?* When we speak of others in our voice do we not displace and appropriate theirs? Is a representation of others free of the play of power and domination in any way possible? Does it all come down to who writes whom? Is colonialism dead? Is it even mortal?

Though we were intensely aware of these issues (even if we formulated them, in those less pensive days, more in methodological than in ethical terms—as questions of rapport) and of the destructive tensions they were inducing in our relations with our hosts, we decided to cut the knot in the Gordian way. Four of us, the three anthropologists from Social Relations together with the sociologist, piled into the chauffeured automobile Ford had provided the project and, asking nobody's leave, headed east, looking for a new site. After canvassing four or five possibilities, we settled on Pare. It was about the right size, had a diverse population and a variegated economy, and, most critically, the district officer in charge of the place was an extraordinary figure, energetic, knowledgeable, supremely self-confident. A local man who, starting as a village policeman, had worked his way up the native wing of the colonial civil service while becoming, at the same time, a strong and active Sukarno nationalist, he very much wanted us to come there. It was also about two hundred kilometers from Jogjakarta: much too far for anyone to commute, much too rustic for anyone to want to.

A declaration of independence, then, almost designed to insult and infuriate. But when we returned to Jogjakarta, full of anxiety over what we had done, and informed the professors that we thought the project should be carried out in the heat and dust of distant Pare rather than the cool greenness of the nearby hill station, their reaction was not only not outraged, but, at least so it seemed, relieved. Apparently, they were by then (this whole episode took seven months to unfold, and this was just about halfway along) as anxious to be free of us, and of responsibility for us, as we were of them; sorry that they had allowed themselves to become involved in so complicated an enterprise in the first place. Their official role in the project became virtually nonexistent, their personal interaction with us grew markedly more relaxed, even warm, and the notion of student counterparts, collective interviewing, and joint reporting simply evaporated. The problem had hardly been solved nor the wounds of confrontation wholly healed. I doubt they ever were. But at least we had moved from active stalemate, taut and ill-tempered, to something rather more resembling limbo.

Just where we now stood, whether the enterprise was off or on, was unclear. We were waiting for the man who had been appointed to replace our lost leader, a young linguist from Yale who had been one of our teachers of Indonesian, to arrive and see whether, as hardly seemed likely, the situation might somehow still be saved. In the meantime we studied Javanese, got to know a great many Jogjanese, and began our inquiries into Javanese culture, hoping that if we were asked to leave, as I at least expected we soon would be, we would be able to patch together some sort of acceptable thesis. It was a difficult time—a world opening up before our eyes and falling from our hands at the same time. But in the end it all proved fortuitous; a gift, in fact, and a godsend. By the time we got to Pare, for of course we finally did get there (the Minister of Culture in Jakarta subjected our hapless new director to a three-hour harangue about arrogance, faithlessness, and the fact that the world was changing and whites had damn better realize it, but ended with, "all right, go to Pare, and the hell with you"), we were already a very long way, over our heads almost, "into the culture."

More than that, we had managed, only half-consciously and without much sense of what it was we really wanted, to shake ourselves free of both the expansive expectations that had sent us to Indonesia and the contracted ones we encountered when we got there. The booming loudspeaker of Harvard seemed a long way off and the preposterous pith-helmet of Gadjah Mada hardly closer. The district officer—he deserves a name (and to my mind a statue): Raden Mas Soemomihardjo—was as good as his word.

He found us local families to live with. He introduced us to anyone we wanted to meet and to many people we hadn't the wit to know that we wanted to meet. He announced to everyone that we had come there because, now that Indonesia was at last independent, Americans needed to know, free of colonial distortions, what its people were really like, and there was, of course, no better place in the entire country to find that out. (A week after I had settled in with the family of a railroad worker, a neighbor asked me, "How many of you are coming? I hear there will be two thousand.") And, most important of all, having done all this, he left us alone. The rest, some two years or so, was, if not exactly history, anyway anthropology. Here, finally, was "the field."

∽

Historicizing yourself, dividing your past into periods, is an uncomfortable sort of thing to do. It is uncomfortable not just for the obvious reason that the further you move from the beginning the closer you come to the end, but because there are so many ways to do it; any particular one seems arbitrary, rooted in very little else but narrative convenience. If you are concerned merely to relate what you've seen and been through that doesn't matter so much. Nobody's under oath in autobiography, whose purpose is normally to keep an illusion in place. But if you are concerned with tracing the movement of a discipline by packaging your experiences into emblematical units it is rather more troubling. You are expected, at least, to justify the units, say what it is the emblems emblematize.

This becomes particularly acute as one approaches the nineteen-sixties. For the one thing that seems generally agreed (which doesn't, of course, in itself make it true) is that, at least in the United States, the sixties were totally different from the fifties—a whole other thing. The fifties were complacent, the sixties torn; the fifties tailored, the sixties scruffy; the fifties well mannered, the sixties confrontational; the fifties silent, the sixties shrill. Vietnam, the civil rights movement, the counterculture were the American *kairos:* the point at which the future changed.

If this story, a product itself of the time it celebrates, is taken at face value, the temptation to see everything in its terms as one moves from considering the Eisenhower era to considering the Kennedy-Johnson one is especially strong. But so far as anthropology is concerned, and indeed the social sciences in general, that doesn't work out very well. Things changed, all right, and significantly. But they changed in ways that were connected more with what was learned, and what unlearned, in the years immediately after the war than with the ambient excitements of the society at large. There was less a fragmentation and a surrender to immediacies (that came later) than a rethinking and a consolidation, the settling in of a general direction.

I spent the sixties at the University of Chicago, arriving as an unformed assistant professor in the fall of 1960, departing as an all-too-formed professor in the spring of 1970: an exact ten years. It was hardly a place remote from the upheavals of the time. There were teach-ins, marches, strikes; the administration building was occupied, professors were physically attacked. Off-campus, the Black Panthers were shot up, the Chicago Seven were tried, the yippies attempted to levitate the Merchandise Mart, and the Democratic convention exploded. Some places, Berkeley, Columbia, Cornell, Kent State, may have had more harrowing moments, and other events, the Cuban missile crisis, the Kennedy and King assassinations, the Watts riots, the fall of Lyndon Johnson, were surely of more lasting significance. But the pervasiveness of the disorder, and its variousness, were hardly anywhere any more thoroughly displayed. If in fact the whole world was watching, it was a very good place to look.

All of this was, of course, much on the minds of the university population. People debated, demonstrated, gave speeches, formed groups, wrote letters to newspapers, or departed for Canada, and there can hardly have been anyone who did not sign a petition. The antiwar protest, to some degree the civil rights movement, rather less the counterculture, engaged much of the energies of faculty and students alike. But they were for the most part, even when on occasion they disrupted the normal flow of things and threw the structures of civility into disarray, rather extra-curricular. The intellectual tone of the university, highly distinctive and rather deep set, half an Arnoldian ideology, half a Burkean morality, really did not alter much. The "sixties" surrounded the place and colored its mood; but only sporadically, and then evanescently, did they invade the workings of its interior life.

That life, as I say, was well established. At least since Robert Maynard Hutchins had agitated the place with his peculiar combination of seriousness and self-promotion in the thirties and forties, and possibly since its first president, William Rainey Harper, had introduced the German idea of the sovereign scholar at the turn of the century, the university had a density and a centeredness not otherwise much found in American academia. For better or worse, it was earnest, purposeful, self-regarding, and intense.

And adventurous. I came to the university as part once more of a wildly multidisciplinary experiment in the social sciences: The Committee for the Comparative Study of New Nations. The Chicago "committee system," by means of which scholarly work could be pursued outside the confines of established departments, especially those Hutchins wished to constrain, circumvent, or even just generally annoy, was already famous, in some quarters infamous. The best-known examples were the Committee on Social Thought, which had been set up, apparently to some degree with his own money, by the economic historian John Nef, and the Ideas and Methods program, which had been organized by the philosopher Richard McKeon, but there were instances scattered throughout the university. The New Nations Committee was conceived by two Chicago professors, the sociologist Edward Shils (who had also been peripherally involved in the Social Relations project at Harvard) and the political scientist David Apter (who had studied at Princeton with one of its more vehement products) in 1958–59 while they were on leave to the Center for Advanced Study in the Behavioral Sciences at Palo Alto—also a recently formed multidisciplinary enterprise. As I, too, was there that year, having just returned from fieldwork in Bali, they asked me to join them in putting their idea in motion, which, after a year of teaching at Berkeley, I did.

In its own way, of course, the Committee was very much a creature of the times. But, focused on understanding the changes consequent upon the collapse of European imperialism after 1945, it was directed outward toward the world in general, not inward toward the domestic malaise. The formation of nearly fifty new states by the early nineteen-sixties, with another fifty promised, virtually all of them in Asia and Africa, virtually all of them weak, instable, poor, and ambitious, seemed to provide a whole new field of inquiry—one in which comparative study could tease out similarities and differences and provide, thereby, guides to intelligent policy. "Realistic, sympathetic studies of the new states," Shils, the Committee's first chairman, wrote in a foundational essay that catches its spirit with an accuracy that now, when benevolence is suspect and confidence hard to come by, seems more than a bit embarrassing.

> Realistic, sympathetic studies of the new states can help to make our policies toward them more understanding, more discriminating, and more helpful. There are benevolent errors to dispel as well as malevolent errors to overcome. We wish to secure the benevolence while dispelling the mythology with which so many well-intentioned persons confront the new states. The differentiated portrayal of the situation of the new states and the subjective and environmental determinants of action might make us, and those who must make policy, more imaginative about the possible lines of development as well as about the obstacles to such development. By a greater realism, coupled with a vivid disclosure of the range of possibilities permitted by the "givens" of life in the new states, and of the capacities of their rulers, we hope also—at least, to some extent—to disarm ill will.

The kind of social research we are practicing is a disciplined extension of experience. The categories we employ are the same as the ones we employ in our studies of our own societies, and they postulate the fundamental affinities of all human beings. Their persistent application in research and the diffusion of the results of research into the circles of influential opinion will, it is hoped, further the process through which that sense of affinity, necessary for constructive policy, is nurtured.

Our undertaking does not, however, intend to attain these moral effects through preaching, exhortation, or manipulation. We seek to do it through enlightenment. Our chosen instrument of enlightenment is systematic research, conducted under the auspices of the best traditions of contemporary social science.

The Committee that was to carry out this formidable enterprise consisted of some thirteen members. (The membership shifted a bit over time.) Two of them were sociologists, three political scientists, five anthropologists, and there were an economist, a lawyer, and a professor of education. Virtually all had carried out field researches in one or another region of the world, most especially West and East Africa, India, and Southeast Asia. Funded by the Carnegie Corporation, the Committee had its own offices and administrative staff, held weekly seminars, organized conferences, supported dissertation write-ups, invited external research fellows, and produced, in the course of time, a fair number of publications. Perhaps Shils's hopes for turning American policy vis-à-vis the Third World toward realism, enlightenment, and sympathetic imagination were somewhat less than completely fulfilled. (This was, again, after all, the time of Katanga, the Tonkin Gulf, Kashmir, and Biafra.) But a scholarly community with a style and a standpoint, something less than a school but more than a talking shop, was nonetheless formed.

So far as my own work was concerned, the task was to develop a research program that could connect both to the Committee's expansive intentions and to my own more circumscribed ones. And this involved the second locus of my Chicago existence, a block away, two stories up, and intellectually enclosed in a quite different world—the Department of Anthropology.

For the first five years at the University I was wholly on the Committee budget; for the last five, independently supported by a Senior Research Career Fellowship from the National Institutes of Mental Health, free to do more or less whatever I wished, if only I could figure out what that might be. But over the whole period I had, as well, an appointment in the anthropology department, and became, almost immediately, deeply engaged, entangled is perhaps a better word, with the more restless of my colleagues there in what turned out, after a while, to be an extremely influential (and extremely controversial) effort to redefine the ethnographical enterprise whole and entire. Known most generally as "symbolic anthropology" (a name bestowed upon it by others elsewhere, and with which I myself have never been entirely happy, if only because it suggests that, like "economic anthropology," "political anthropology," or "the anthropology of religion," it is a specialty or a subdiscipline rather than a foundational critique of the field as such), this redefinition consisted in placing the systematic study of meaning, the vehicles of meaning, and the understanding of meaning at the very center of research and analysis: to make of anthropology, or anyway cultural anthropology, a hermeneutical discipline.

We would not, of course, have then called it that, for the term, and the movement, was largely unknown in the United States, and when known, suspected as European, literary, or worse, philosophical. But that is what it was. In the course of a thoroughgoing overhaul of the curriculum and the institution of a new set of required introductory courses in the graduate program, courses designed to convey to doctoral candidates what we expected of them, the faculty found itself driven beyond the boundaries of the received traditions in anthropology to a consideration of more general intellectual trends—trends which in the following decades would, under such rubrics as the linguistic, the interpretive, the social constructionist, the new historicist, the rhetorical, or the semiotic "turn," become increasingly powerful in all the human sciences. Doubtless, much of our thought was fumbling and undeveloped. Certainly, hardly any of it was unmarked by quarrel. But "the move toward meaning" has proved a proper revolution: sweeping, durable, turbulent, and consequential.

However that may be, I was, for my part, projected by all of this into an all-consuming, but after Harvard not unfamiliar, preoccupation: how to arrange these various elements—the Committee's vision of a new field of study, the ethnographers' reconceptualization of their professional task, and my own concern, brought along with me vaguely from my liberal arts past, with the role of thought in history—into a practicable program of empirical research. Once again, only the pressures of fieldwork seemed capable of sorting out a scramble of ideas. By going someplace, different and distant, and staying there awhile, one could make up one's mind. Or, perhaps more exactly, have it made up for one.

There were, however, some problems rather more immediate. The sixties in Indonesia were even more explosive than in America or Europe, and in the middle of them the massacres erupted. With two children, both under five, returning there seemed a dubious proposition. Even had I risked it, or gone alone (I have never worked in the field alone for more than a month or so, and doubt very much that I could have managed it), it seems unlikely that the government, that is, the army, would have allowed me to move about with the requisite freedom, or, even if it had, that anyone would have been comfortable talking to me. I was reduced, as I had been in those first flustered years at Harvard, to that most pitiable of conditions: an anthropologist without a people.

And, as in those years, I floundered about for some time trying to imagine where I might go, never mind what I might do were I in fact actually to get there. I considered Bengal for a while. Perhaps I could find a Hindu town with a Muslim minority on the Indian side of the border and a Muslim one with a Hindu minority on the, as it was then, East Pakistan side; a balanced contrast for a reciprocal comparison—by this time an almost instinctive way of going at things for me. But, though I went so far as to study

Bengali for a couple of months, that tense, fever-ridden region, moving toward an explosion of its own, was hardly more plausible an idea just then than was collapsing Java, and I soon gave it up. For an uneasy, uncertain period, I continued to drift, writing retrospectively about Indonesia, thinking prospectively, and not very exactly, of all sorts of elsewheres: the Philippines, Uganda, Suriname, Bosnia, Madagascar.

All this indefiniteness and indecision were, once again, resolved suddenly, in a way wholly unexpected, by a possibility wholly unforeseen. In the summer of 1963, a sort of summit conference, designed to reduce what was felt to be a marked difference in approach between what the British called "Social Anthropology" and the Americans called "Cultural Anthropology," a difference the appearance of "symbolic anthropology" (again, not another branch of anthropology, but another notion of what anthropology was) seemed, if anything, to be deepening, was held at Cambridge University. The nature of this Anglo-American mis-meeting of minds, having to do at base with a stress on concrete, "real as a seashell" social relationships and institutions on the empiricist Anglo side as against "shreds and patches" agglomerations of customs and thought-ways on the historicist American one, is no longer of any particular relevance, now that these matters are (in most places) less simplistically conceived. Nor, to my mind, was the debate as important then as the champions of either party, decided, dug in, and overly articulate, imagined it to be. But it was, nonetheless, noticeably heated, obstructive in the way only academic opinion-peddling, especially when large reputations are involved, can be, and the conference was planned as an attempt to get beyond it.

The degree to which it was successful in this can be judged by others; historians, perhaps, absorbed in the passions of ancient quarrels. I found it, as I suppose most summiteers do once the excitement of sensing oneself to be at the center of things passes, somehow both a portentous, transforming event, a sea change in something, and one curiously unproductive of observable movement. However that may be, the meeting's effect on me was to accentuate my desperation to get away from lecture halls and meeting rooms, and the sort of people one found there, and into the field. During the course of it, at some intermission in some pub or other, I poured out my "where next?" anxieties to one of the younger and less over-socialized British participants—I can, alas, no longer remember who it was—and he said, "You should go to Morocco: it is safe, it is dry, it is open, it is beautiful, there are French schools, the food is good, and it is Islamic." The logical force of this argument, bereft as it was of scientific argumentation, was so overwhelming that, immediately the conference ended, I flew to Morocco rather than returning to Chicago. I drove about the country talking to various sorts of officials and looking at various sorts of walls, gates, minarets, and alleyways for several weeks, and decided on the spot and with almost nothing in the way of either plan or rationale—it *was* beautiful and it *was* Islamic—to organize a long-term, multi-researcher study there. The Java Project, II.

Sequels have a way, however, of wandering off course and more mocking their originals than replicating them, particularly when they are constructed at other times, by other people, to other ends. Not only had the *après guerre* elation of the fifties pretty well evaporated by 1963 when I took my flying trip through Morocco's countryside (itself not unreminiscent of that desperate journey through east central Java), but what had looked, at the earlier period, to be a slow but inevitable convergence of theories and techniques began to look, by the latter one, to be an equally slow but equally inevitable differentiation of them. This had, at least for me, an exhilaration of its own, for I have always thought that understanding social life entails not an advance toward an omega point, "Truth," "Reality," "Being," or "the World," but the restless making and unmaking of facts and ideas. But it did mean that research planning was hardly any longer a straightforward matter—set the goal, outline the procedure, mobilize the resources. *On s'engage, puis on voit,* plunge in and see what happens, seemed much more in order.

Two critical changes from the Java format seemed dictated by the very nature of things; those famous "material conditions of anthropological production." First, in the absence of the sort of large-scale funding and developed administrative context that had been available to the Java project, and indeed imposed upon it, a simultaneous, multi-pronged attack by nine or ten people seemed out of the question, particularly if I did not want, as I emphatically did not want, to become a full-time project administrator, fund raiser, and research planner, rather than, once again, a researcher among researchers. Building houses for other people to live in simply didn't attract. I wanted to get something going, but I wanted it then to run by itself.

Second, I was not at this point part of a multidisciplinary department, as I had been before and would be subsequently; I would have to draw my colleagues from among anthropology doctoral students looking, as I had been looking a decade earlier, for a thesis and for a field site in which to produce one. (The Committee for the Comparative Study of New Nations was interdisciplinary in terms of its members, all of whom had regular faculty appointments in standard departments as their main locus of work, and of course in outlook, but it had no students, no research program, and no resources to sponsor field expeditions.) The confinement of whatever group I formed to anthropologists was not in itself so great a departure from the Java project, in that, of those originally involved, all, save for a single sociologist who was really an anthropologist in disguise, who finally made it to Pare were in fact anthropologists—the clinical psychologist, social psychologist, historian, and so on peeling off at various points, for various reasons. But it did mean that if the study of Sefrou, the site I chose to be, in my mind anyway, Pare's counterpart, was to escape the established agendas of anthropology and become something rather less parochial, multidisciplinary in mind-set if not in professional identity, I would have to contrive somehow or other to see that it did.

Given, then, that a simultaneous descent upon the field site by several hands was contraindicated for both practical and intellectual considerations (looking back, the Pare study seemed, even after a good deal of the original apparatus had been sheared away in our break with Gadjah Mada, a bit *too* concentrated, *too* intense—a lower profile had certain advantages), I decided to try a chain-link approach. My wife and I would go to Sefrou for a year or so, a doctoral student, with whom we would overlap only for a month or two in the field for orientation purposes, would then come for a year or so, we would return for another year a month or so before the student left to return to Chicago, and so on. In general, this plan was put into effect and, in general, it worked quite well. My wife and I, together with three doctoral candidates succeeding one another in time, our stays interspersed between theirs and bracketing them, kept Sefrou more or less "covered" between 1965 and 1971.

In the end, I don't know that, for all the contrasts in academic tone between Harvard and Chicago (The Sociology Is About to Begin; Meaning Matters) and in general mood between the fifties and the sixties (The American Century; Where Have All the Young Men Gone?), the two projects, one an attempt to rationalize social research along industrial lines, the other a more patched-together handicraft affair, worked out so very differently in practice. "The Field" itself is, or at least it was in these two cases, a powerful disciplinary force: assertive, demanding, even coercive. Like any such force, it can be underestimated or otherwise occluded, and by some individuals in either case was. But it cannot, at least if one is not going to disengage altogether, as in both cases some individuals did, be simply evaded. It is too insistent for that.

The difficulty, as every anthropologist who has tried to do it knows, is that it is virtually impossible to convey what precisely the nature of this discipline is, or even where exactly it comes from. Some of us try analogies. (My own favorite, though I don't think it has ever worked, is a chess game, with the traditionalized positional moves of the opening game as one gets settled, finds people to work with, and so on; the complex, harder-to-standardize combinations of the middle game when one launches probes in all sorts of directions and tries, once they are out there and probing, to relate them to

one another; and the sterner, more formalized mopping up procedures of the minimalist end game.) Others try lengthy, boring, and
wholly inadequate descriptions of how they lived, what they ate,
how they kept fieldnotes, whom they interviewed; appending,
perhaps, inventories, schedules, lists of questions. More recently
there have been some attempts to depict fieldwork experience in
autobiographical terms (one of them emerged from the Morocco
project), and they have had their interest. But somehow they lead
more to rumination and self-inspection, and to a curious inte-
riorization of what is in fact an intensely public activity, than they
do to an ordered account of what field research comes to as a
mode of inquiry. Like psychoanalysts mumbling about "working
through," we lack the language to articulate what takes place when
we are in fact at work. There seems to be a genre missing.

What emerges, in my account as in others, reminds me of an
old Red Skelton movie, whose title I no longer remember. Skelton
is a hack writer of adventure stories for boys. Pacing up and down,
he is dictating to an amanuensis. "Wonder Boy was trapped in the
tent. All around him were circling Indians. The prairie had been
set on fire. He had no more bullets. All his food was gone. Night
was coming. How would Wonder Boy get out of the tent? End of
Chapter 22." A pause, while Skelton collects his thoughts. Then:
"Chapter 23. After Wonder Boy got out of the tent . . ."

⌇

After I left Chicago, the Moroccan project established and functioning, I found myself in the most unstandard, and the most
difficult, academic environment yet: the Institute for Advanced
Study in Princeton, New Jersey. The Institute, which was founded
in 1930 on the basis of an endowment from a New Jersey department store family, was intended by its projector and first director,
the philanthropical entrepreneur and all-round fixer of things
Abraham Flexner, to be America's answer to Oxford's All Souls
and Paris's Collège de France, as well as a haven for eminent
scholars and scientists fleeing fascist Europe. Flexner, who was by

then in his mid-sixties, with a trail of triumphs and resignations stretched out behind him, was not given to shaded views and small thoughts:

> Progress might be greatly assisted [he wrote a year or so before launching the Institute] by the outright creation of a school or institute of higher learning . . . It should be a free society of scholars—free, because mature persons, animated by intellectual purposes, must be left to pursue their own ends in their own way. Administration should be slight and inexpensive. Scholars and scientists should participate in its government; the president should come down from his pedestal. The term "organization" should be banned. The institution should be open to persons, competent and cultivated, who do not need and would abhor spoon feeding . . . It should furnish simple surroundings—books, laboratories, and above all tranquility—absence of distraction either by worldly concerns or by parental responsibility for an immature student body. Provision should be made for the amenities of life in the institution and in the private life of the staff. It need not be complete or symmetrical: if a chair could not be admirably filled, it should be left vacant. There exists in America no university in this sense—no institution, no seat of learning devoted to higher teaching and research. Everywhere the pressure of undergraduate and vocational activities hampers the serious objects for which universities exist . . . science and scholarship suffer; money is wasted . . .
>
> What could be expected, if a modern American university were thus established? The ablest scholars and scientists would be attracted to its faculty; the most earnest students would be attracted to its laboratories and seminars. It would be small . . . but its propulsive power would be momentous out of all proportion to its size. It would, like a lens, focus rays that now scatter . . .

This sort of talk appears less often in public discourse these days, when the charge of elitism is so powerful a delegitimizing force. One does not speak so airily, and certainly not so frankly, of faculty amenities and the world-avoiding life. But it not only expresses the outlook that launched the Institute in the first place; it expresses the spirit, or the ideology, that, stated and restated by faculty, directors, and trustees alike, from that day to this, continues to animate it.

Or at least, supposedly so. From the very beginning, the idealized nature of such a picture of the ultimate academy, a place where mind met mind and passion, self, and ignorance were absent, came under a certain amount of question. When Flexner wrote to one of his early advisors, Felix Frankfurter, that the Institute was "a paradise for scholars," Frankfurter, who, whatever else he may have been, was rather fully in the world, responded:

> [I do not] think it very helpful to take too seriously the exuberant rhetoric of thinking of the Institute as a "paradise for scholars." For one thing, the natural history of paradise is none too encouraging a precedent. Apparently it was an excellent place for one person, but it was fatal even for two—or at least for two when the snake entered, and the snake seems to be an early and congenial companion of man . . . Let's try to aim at something human, for we are dealing with humans and not with angels.

It did not take long to make Frankfurter a prophet (and an ex-advisor). Alongside Flexner's transcendent scholars tranquilly conversing in simple surroundings, an image reinforced by some notable early appointments, Hermann Weyl, John von Neumann, Erwin Panofsky, Kurt Godel, and of course most famously, Albert Einstein (whose own view of Princeton seems to have been—as he wrote in a letter to the Queen of Belgium—that it was "a quaint and ceremonious village of puny demigods on stilts"), there developed the sort of highly personalized academic politics such a collection of luminaries set free from real-world constraints to rub up against one another might be expected to produce.

Flexner soon found out, as he should already have known, that, when it comes to immaturity, students are scarcely a patch on professors. He not only had to come down from his pedestal but, in a fit of faculty opposition, he was driven from the garden altogether, forced to resign. A series of bitter, what's mine is mine, what's yours is negotiable quarrels led to chronic discord—quarrels over appointments, quarrels over the formation of schools within the Institute (one in Political Economy was disbanded altogether; the "sciences" split, not without pain, into Mathematics and Natural Sciences; the school of Humanistic Studies evolved, if that's the word for what seems to have been a tortuous change of mind, into the school of Historical Studies), and, of course, quarrels over salaries, then as now too small for demigods, too large for publication. Tensions between faculty and directors, directors and trustees, and trustees and faculty, as well as between all of them and the philanthropist who had endowed the institution in the first place and had begun to wonder whether he and his sister should have founded instead the medical school Flexner had talked them out of, developed and spread. The national, Cold War controversies in which the third Director, Robert Oppenheimer, found himself caught up during the nineteen-fifties, especially since his chief antagonist, Lewis Strauss, the chairman of the Atomic Energy Commission, was on the Institute Board of Trustees and had invited him to be Director in the first place, made something of a mockery of the far from the madding crowd view of intellectual life. *Et in arcadia ego:* the rays that Flexner wanted focused got more than a little interferential.

All this internal warfare was, as far as I was concerned, so much prehistory when I arrived in 1970, innocent of any knowledge of it and unacquainted with any of my instant colleagues, to be the first professor in yet another new school in the Institute—Social Science. But it rather soon became clear that if past is prologue anywhere, it is at the Institute, which less transcends its crises than, reproducing its culture with a fidelity that would make the Tibetans envious, reenacts them. The Director then, and the originator of the proposal for such a school, was the economist Carl Kaysen, who had himself been appointed only a few years before, and his efforts met with what can only be called unbuttoned hostility from a good part of the faculty and buttoned hostility from much of the rest. "Social science will be your Viet Nam," a particularly *enragé* mathematician told Kaysen. "Yours will be a Pyrrhic victory," he told me, who was taken aback to hear that I had, accidentally, enlisted in a war. (He also quoted Abbé Sieyès about the *tiers état*.

I didn't quite get the force of this; don't to this day. But he was clearly up on his martial imagery.) It was not exactly a comfortable beginning.

But it was nothing in comparison with what was to come: "The Bellah Affair." When I was appointed, via an external ad hoc committee of social scientists, there was, as yet, no school, but a preliminary "program" of five or six one-year visitors, run essentially out of Kaysen's office. For the first two years I struggled to find my feet in what I soon discovered was an extremely tense and increasingly obsessive community—skeptical of the social sciences, suspicious of me, and outright paranoid about Kaysen. In order to get things moving toward permanent institutionalization, which I understood I had been brought there to do, in the fall of 1972 I nominated, with Kaysen's support, a leading sociologist, Robert Bellah, to be the second professor. Bellah, Ford Professor of Sociology at the University of California, Berkeley, was a specialist on Japan, on comparative religion, and on large-scale social change. He had been a student in the Social Relations Department at Harvard when I was there in the fifties, and, though we had never actually worked together and had not seen much of one another in the interim, I had long been impressed with his breadth of learning and, something not entirely common in the social sciences, his moral seriousness.

With his nomination, however, all hell broke loose. For nearly two years the Institute was convulsed in a struggle so bitter that it became, with the assistance of some professors with a developed gift for malignant eloquence, a defective sense of decency, and underground connections to the press, a cause célèbre of, at least for academia, major proportions—an *"Affaire"* indeed. The "paradise" image, apparently indestructible, returned to haunt us, and— the wages of privilege are *Schadenfreude*—we found ourselves faced with a series of mocking headlines: "Trouble in Paradise," "Ivory Tower Tempest," "Thunderbolts on Olympus," "The Garden of the Lonely Wise," "In the Groves Where Einstein Toiled . . . the Dialog Isn't Socratic," "Infighting in the Ivory Tower,"

"Einstein Is a Hard Act to Follow," and "Bad Days on Mt. Olympus." ("The posse was made up of geniuses, mostly," the story under the last one began. "Tried to run the sheriff out of town. Didn't do it but they sure shot up the old Intellectual Hotel.") As the furor mounted, what had started out as a straightforward matter exploded, dignity be damned, justice though the heavens fall, into sheer unreason. Comity, such as it was, collapsed altogether; and the whole institution came perilously close to collapsing with it.

The gory details of the happenings that followed, which seemed to me more of a collective temper tantrum than a responsible effort to determine the worth of Bellah, the value of his appointment, or the future of the Institute, need not again be recounted. The press at the time is there for those attracted to academic pathologies, and I am hardly a neutral witness. Suffice it to say that the outcome of the agony—Bellah's most acutely, for he was treated with a cruelty of particular exquisiteness; Kaysen's most deeply, for the internal attacks upon him were loutish, loud, and above all relentless; and mine, derivatively, for having inadvertently brought all this to pass and, reasonably enough I suppose, being left somehow to cope with it—was that Bellah was appointed over the opposition of a majority of the faculty but, partly as a result of a personal tragedy, returned to his position at Berkeley, the School of Social Science was formally constituted by the Board of Trustees, and Kaysen, wearied of being harassed, left the Institute. It wasn't exactly the Pyrrhic victory my learned colleague had promised me, for all was, as it turned out, far from lost. But I did feel a bit under siege.

The siege has never really lifted in the decades since. (Almost twenty years to the day, the Bellah affair was virtually reenacted, this time mercifully without the attentions of the press, in connection with another proposed appointment to the school.) Eternal vigilance remains the price of liberty; the expectant optimism of Harvard in the fifties and the searching earnestness of Chicago in the sixties are, by now, but memories of a different existence. But, partly as a result of a mere refusal to go away and leave the stilt-walkers in peace, partly as a result of support from a few sympathetic and fair-minded figures among the faculty and a few more among the Board of Trustees, and most of all, I think, because the Institute as such had, like Nietzsche, looked into the abyss and the abyss had looked back, the School, now that it was officially founded, grew and, in spite of it all, prospered. In 1974 Albert Hirschman, an economist, was appointed as the second professor; in 1980 Michael Walzer, a political theorist, was appointed as the third; and in 1985 Joan Scott, a social historian, was appointed as the fourth.

There is more, however, to forming a school than making appointments. The rationale, insofar as there is one, for a permanent faculty in a place such as the Institute is less in giving twenty or twenty-five supposedly gifted people the opportunity to work as they will at whatever they will than in establishing and sustaining an intellectual environment in which mathematics or physics or history . . . or social science . . . can flourish and advance. The hundred and fifty or so research fellows (fifteen to twenty in the social sciences) who come to the Institute each year to work on a project of some sort or other are, in my view anyway, the heart of the matter. If Flexner's magnification of propulsive power, his focusing of dispersed rays, is to come about, it is through them that it will for the most part happen. The permanent faculty can develop initiatives. It can set courses and encourage talents. It can explore directions. It can hardly in itself bring them to fruition.

With such a view of the job those of us who have been called permanently to the Institute are, beyond the pursuit of our separate obsessions, there to perform, there are a number of matters that need to be decided. Of these, by far the most important is how to relate a very small, not especially representative, modestly funded operation to the magnificent hodgepodge of ideas and activities—International Social Science—it is supposed to enrich. It is impossible to replicate the large in the little, to reflect all the disciplines in all their currents, or even the bulk of them. There is just too much out there. It is necessary to establish a particular domain, angle, style, standpoint—I'm not sure what, precisely, it ought to be called: an attitude, maybe, a vision, perhaps—within the collection of fields, studies, projects, and the like which present themselves to the world as social science, and see what one can do with that. Yet it is necessary, too, if the enterprise is not to become a parochial sideshow, wandering off in some vagrant direction, isolated, irrelevant, and self-admiring, to connect its work to what's happening—to general movements, general problems, general achievements. It is this dilemma, how to lay a course distinct enough to come to something and connected enough to have an impact beyond itself, how, however slightly, to move the hodge-podge, that has animated the school and determined its form. It has been constructed, like anything that didn't exist before, in the middle of things that for a long while have.

The overall direction that has been taken is again a generally "interpretive" one—the sort of thing I encountered in various stages of development at Harvard and Chicago and have pursued since, and that the other members of the school faculty encountered in other forms, in other disciplines, with other implications, in other contexts. We are hardly of one mind on everything and we have different interests and different problems before us; but we are all suspicious of casting the social sciences in the image of the natural sciences, and of general schemes which explain too much. We have sought, rather, to advance a conception of research centered on the analysis of the significance of social actions for those who carry them out and of the beliefs and institutions that lend to those actions that significance. Human beings, gifted with language and living in history, are, for better or worse, possessed of intentions, visions, memories, hopes, and moods, as well as of passions and judgments, and these have more than a little to do with what they do and why they do it. An attempt to understand their social and cultural life in terms of forces, mechanisms, and drives alone, objectivized variables set in systems of closed causality, seems unlikely of success.

That, in any case, is the course we have worked out in the school over the years. It has placed us not so much in direct opposition to mainstream social science, which remains fairly well bound to received ideas as to what counts as evidence, knowledge, explanation, and proof. It places us at some oblique and questioning angle to it: wary, restless, and unconforming. The proper stance, perhaps, for so anomalous an undertaking in so peculiar a place.

The problem of relating our beleaguered storefront venture to the grand march of the social sciences was made all the more severe by the fact that the philosophical disquietudes that had been gathering within those sciences during the previous two decades grew so powerful in the seventies and eighties as to disarrange their sense of what it was they were all about; where it was the march was going. It was not just that the enterprise lost cohesion. It had never been—Durkheim, Weber, Marshall, Simmel—that well integrated. Nor was it that it was suddenly beset by the clash of discordant voices. The polemical stance—Marx, Freud, Malinowski, Pareto—had always been prominent. It was that the foundations upon which the social science idea had rested since anyway the time of Comte shifted, weakened, wobbled, slipped away. The moral and epistemological vertigo that struck the culture generally in the post-structuralist, post-modernist, post-humanist age, the age of turns and texts, of the evaporated subject and the constructed fact, struck the social sciences with particular force.

The story of all this, told in different ways with different morals, and dropping a particular selection of the famous names, Nietzsche or Benjamin to Kuhn or Derrida, has been traced already too many times and is far too intricate for capsule summary, and it is anyway still very much in motion. But its expression within anthropology, where, once again, I happened onto it, or it onto me, has taken by now a reasonably determinate form focused about a handful of radical anxieties so intimately interconnected as to be but restatements of one another: a worry about the legitimacy of speaking for others, a worry about the distorting effects of Western assumptions on the perception of others, and a worry about the ambiguous involvements of language and authority in the depiction of others. Taken together they have seemed to some—but not to me, still working away at my instructive odd couple—to undermine the very idea of comparative ethnography trained upon difference.

The nervousness about speaking for others grows out of the introspections induced in anthropologists by the massive decolonization after the Second World War. That most of the classic field studies were carried out in colonial or semi-colonial settings, settings in which being white and Western conferred in itself a certain privilege and involved, willy-nilly, a certain complicity, has raised questions of the right of the politically dominant to articulate the beliefs and desires of those they dominate. The history of ethnography, or so anyway it has come to be argued, is one of the appropriation of the voices of the weak by those of the strong, much as their labor or their natural resources were appropriated by more straightforward imperialists; and this, so also it is argued, ill-fits it to play its self-assigned (and self-congratulatory) role of the tribune of such voices in the contemporary world. Compromised in its origins, it is compromised in its acts—ventriloquizing others, making off with their words.

The second concern, that about the inability of anthropologists, most of them American, British, German, or French, and virtually all of them Western trained, to free themselves from views derived from their own culture so as to see other peoples "in their own terms," is but the worry about occluding other voices expressed in an epistemological key. If the frames of meaning upon which we depend to find our own way about in life are so deeply ingrained in us as to color our every perception, it is difficult to see how our accounts of what others feel or think or do, to say nothing of our theories about them, can be anything but sheer imposition. Imposition and systematic distortion: "orientalism," "cultural hegemony," "symbolic domination"—the ethnographic claim to knowledge is everywhere put into a moral shadow, redescribed as an impress of power.

All this doubt and meta-doubt is completed and made seemingly

inescapable by the viewing of social science discourse, anthropological or any other, as politically charged, shot through with
implicit claims to mastery and control. The capacity of language
to construct, if not reality "as such" (whatever that is), at least
reality as everyone engages it in actual practice—named, pictured,
catalogued, and measured—makes of the question of who describes whom, and in what terms, a far from indifferent business.
If there is no access to the world unmediated by language (or
anyway by sign systems) it rather matters what sort of language
that is. Depiction is power. The representation of others is not
easily separable from the manipulation of them.

If one is not simply to surrender to these anxieties and declare
anthropology impossible or, worse, oppressive (and some, indeed,
have done just that), it is insufficient just to press on regardless.
The view, favored among "back to real anthropology" traditionalists, that the absorption with such matters is but the product of
fashion and will soon dissolve, is quite wrong—itself a fashion,
worn and outmoded. It is simply the condition of things that
anthropology, like social science in general, is a far more difficult
line of work, difficult and uncomfortable, now that the "we define,
they are defined" assumptions that sustained and guided it in its
forming phases have been brought into question. There is a need
for extensive revisions of our notions as to what anthropology is,
what its aims should be, what it can reasonably hope to accomplish; why it is anyone should pursue it. If the relation of what we
write to what we write about, Morocco, say, or Indonesia, can no
longer be credibly compared with that of a map to a distant
territory hitherto uncharted or to that of a sketch to an exotic
animal recently come upon, what can it be compared with? Telling
a believable story? Building a workable model? Translating an
alien language? Construing an enigmatical text? Conducting an
intelligible dialogue? Excavating a buried site? Advancing a moral
cause? Restructuring a political debate? Staging an instructive
illusion? All these possibilities and more have been suggested and
counter-suggested; but the only thing that seems certain is that the
game has changed.

Once again, however, these transformations in outlook and attitude, in anthropologists' sense of what they are up to and what they should expect to gain from it, are not mere conceptual changes, driven on by the pure dialectic of theoretical debate, which doesn't play that great a role in anthropology in any case. They are changes in the way in which anthropology is practiced, driven on by alterations in the concrete circumstances under which research is conducted. It is not just ideas that are no longer what they were. The world isn't either.

The end of colonialism, or anyway the formal end of it whatever aftershadows remain in the minds of both former masters and former subjects, has produced more than the realization that classical ethnographical accounts were affected by the privileged position of the ethnographer in the larger scheme of things. It has produced, now that the scheme has altered and the privilege departed (*that* sort of privilege, anyway), an extensive change in everything from our access to field sites and our standing vis-à-vis those we work with within them to our relationships with other fields of inquiry and our overall schedule of interests. We work now neither in sheltered settings nor in set-apart ones, enclaves and outliers left—subject to considerations of "reason and morality" and whatever they might contribute to imperial trade—to their own devices. We work in intensely contested ones among all sorts of constrictions, demands, suspicions, and competitors.

Changes in the readiness of access are the most directly felt of the alterations in the circumstances of research. Under the Shah field study boomed; under Khomeini it virtually disappeared. Indonesia has been a yes, a no, and then again a yes proposition; Morocco has become a haven for ethnographers shut out of much of the rest of the Arab world. Tanzania and Thailand are, for the moment, crowded with researchers; Ethiopia and Burma are largely absent of them. Papua is dangerous; Sri Lanka is worse. But even when access is relatively speaking easy (it is not absolutely speaking easy anywhere, now that Governors General and Native Affairs Officers are a thing of the past), the relations with those one is studying become touchier and more difficult to navigate.

When you are there as a petitioning visitor in a sovereign country dealing with people whose country it is and when, though I myself have never experienced it, you are there under the administrative aegis and political shield of an imperial power, personal relations work out rather differently. There may be new asymmetries, stemming from everything from economic disparity to the international balance of military force, but the old ones, arbitrary, fixed, and rigidly unilateral, are pretty well gone.

And beyond these more immediate matters there are a number of other alterations in the conditions of ethnographic work. First, such work is now almost never undertaken in places where other sorts of scholars are not present, or at least nearby: historians, economists, philologists, political scientists, sociologists, psychologists, art fanciers, filmmakers, musicologists, even now and then a philosopher or two. And journalists, of course, are everywhere. The day when ethnographers were intellectual masters of all they surveyed from child raising and trade to cosmology and house-building, if only because they were about the only people who went to such places to study such things, are long gone. We work now under the critical gaze of, and sometimes in harness with, a very wide range of other sorts of specialists. (Indeed, an increasing number of us work on Western societies, and even our own; a move which simplifies some matters and complicates others.)

Second, not all ethnographers, by far, now are Western. Not only is there usually a significant contingent of local anthropologists, some of them of international standing—as is the case for both Indonesia and Morocco—but even in the West the profession is no longer a monopoly of Americans and Europeans. Individuals from African, Asian, and Latin American backgrounds, as well as by now Native American, have joined its ranks. The critical gaze from neighboring disciplines is supplemented by a similar gaze, even more searching, from within our own.

And finally, our sheer numbers have burgeoned. When I entered graduate school in 1950, there were about two thousand members of the American Anthropological Association; by 1992 there were well over ten thousand, and the end is not in sight. If one were to measure, as I have not the heart to do, the rate of publication and the subjects covered, the contrast would be even more alarming. Once a guild occupation, comparing itself alternately to a tribe, a craft, or a social club, anthropology has become a sprawling consortium of dissimilar scholars held together largely by will and convenience.

The two decades I have spent at the Institute have been, thus, less a matter of tooling up to go somewhere or finding something comparative to do (I already had my sites, and my projects were ongoing, a pendulum cycle of seeming eternal return), than of trying to locate my abiding interests—in meaning, in understanding, and in forms of life—within an increasingly unsettled intellectual field. The unsettledness is hardly limited to anthropology, of course, but, in one form or another, is perfectly general in the human sciences. (Even economics has begun to squirm; even art history.) With nearly four hundred people having come, fifteen or twenty at a time, through it for a year, our irregular school has proved an excellent place to observe the commotion and try out ways of staying upright within it. Learning to exist in a world quite different from that which formed you is the condition, these days, of pursuing research you can on balance believe in and writing sentences you can more or less live with. Settling in at a crossroads of controversy, artfully designed to make contentment difficult, is, it turns out, a very good way of doing that.

❧

I learn by going, the poet Theodore Roethke once wrote, though he was talking about something else, where I have to go. Becoming an anthropologist is not, or anyway has not been for me, an induction into an established profession, like law, medicine, or the flying of airplanes, already there, graded and subdivided, waiting to hammer one into slot-ready shape. My wandering among programs, projects, committees, and institutes, with only the odd stop-off at anthropology departments, is admittedly a bit unstandard; not a recipe everyone will find attractive. But the picture of a career less followed than assembled, put together in the course of effecting it, is not now so altogether unusual.

The sequence of settings into which you are projected as you go if not forward at least onward, thoroughly uncertain of what awaits, does far more to shape the pattern of your work, to discipline it and give it form, than do theoretical arguments, methodological pronouncements, canonized texts, or even, as are these days too much with us, left and right, iron commitments to intellectual creeds. These things matter (perhaps more to some people than they do to me), but it is what you find before you—an eclectic collection of let's-get-on-with-it enthusiasts at *après guerre* Harvard; a tense, ideology-ridden society, hurtling toward violence, in post-Independence Indonesia; an equanimous company of long-distance reasoners amid the political tumult of sixties Chicago; an ancient community beset by sociological blur and cultural self-questioning in reemerged Morocco; a carefully defended island of specialistic research in manicured Princeton—that most powerfully directs your intellectual trajectory. You move less between thoughts than between the occasions and predicaments that bring them to mind.

This is not to say that the whole thing is but a chapter of accidents. Such a view of what purports, after all, to be a scientific career devoted to finding out things thought to be so and persuading others that at least they might be, involves distortions of its own not unselfserving. For surely it can't be the case—can it?—that the merest stumbling about, passively noting what strikes one as notable, is sufficient to accomplish so exacting a task. In the course of all this coming and going and knocking about surely there emerge some governing aims continuously worked toward, some practiced skills habitually exercised, some determinate standards repeatedly applied, some settled judgments as to what is knowable and what isn't, what will work and what won't, what matters and what doesn't. Representing what one has been doing as the result of just about everything in the world except one's beliefs and intentions—"it just happened"—is hardly plausible, a

6

Modernities

he commanding categories of Western history, the words that
ke our worlds go round—Antiquity, the Middle Ages, the Ren-
ance, the Reformation, the Enlightenment, Romanticism—have
n succeeded in this century, and especially since the First World
r, by another no less sovereign: Modernity. Modern is what
ne of us think we are, others of us wish desperately to be, yet
ers despair of being, or regret, or oppose, or fear, or, now, desire
nehow to transcend. It is our universal adjective. There is mod-
art, modern science, modern philosophy, modern society, mod-
politics, modern technology, modern history, modern culture,
dern medicine, modern sex, modern religion, the modern mind,
dern women, and modern war. Modernity, or its absence, sets
nomies, regimes, peoples, and moralities off from one another;
es them generally in the calendar of our time.

But though it is, originally, a Western word and a Western notion
first appears in the sixteenth century, in its late Latin meaning
"now existing," "of this time"), the idea of modernity has
come the common property of all the world, even more prized
I puzzled over in Asia, Africa, and Latin America, where it is
isidered to be just now, perhaps, at last arriving, or, for various
ts of dark reasons, still not doing so, than in Europe and North
ierica, where it is regarded as being, for better or worse, largely
place. Whatever it is, it is pervasive, as either a presence or a

way of removing oneself from the picture in
oneself into it.

Since the decline, in most quarters, of be.
sovereign scientific method and the associated
to be had by radically objectivizing the proce
has become harder and harder to separate what
from the side of the investigator from what cor
side of the investigated. In anthropology, in ai
case anyway, assuming either has anything to d
indivisible experience of trying to find my feet ii
and of the places themselves pressing themselv
to have produced whatever has appeared und
signature. Indeed, it has produced that signatui

lack, an achievement or a failure, a liberation or a burden. Whatever it is.

One thing it may be is a process, a sequence of occurrences that
transforms a traditional form of life, stable and self-contained, into
a venturous one, adaptive and continuously changing, and it is as
such, as *modernization,* that it has appeared in the social sciences.
Weber, Marx, Durkheim, even Adam Smith, were all obsessed with
the energy introduced into Western society (and, in their time, only
Western society), by capitalism, by the industrial and scientific
revolutions, and by the exploration and impressment of the rest
of the world. The way we live now is a stage in a vast historical
proceeding with an intrinsic dynamic, a settled direction, and a
determinate form. They did not altogether agree as to what the
dynamic, direction, and form were. Neither did those who followed them. Neither do we. But that modernization (and thus
modernity, its goal and product) is a general phenomenon unevenly realized has not until recently been very much questioned.

When the colonial system in its classical form, wealth-collecting
metropoles carrying off products from wealth-yielding possessions,
began to break down during and after the Second World War, the
relation between countries in which industrialism, science, and the
like had settled in and those in which they had not had to be
phrased in a more forward-looking way. And for that, the modernization idea seemed especially well made, convenient at once to
ex-masters and ex-subjects anxious to restate their inequalities in
a hopeful idiom. There were advanced (developed, dynamic, rich,
innovative, dominant) societies which had been modernized, and
there were backward (underdeveloped, static, poor, hidebound,
dominated) ones which had not, or not yet, and the challenge,
surely one the determined application of intelligence could meet,
was seen as turning the second into the first. The whole pattern
of global connections was reformulated in these terms—as an
effort to "close the gap," bring the world up to speed.

The spread of this sort of developmentalism was intense and
rapid in almost all the "new nations"—certainly in Indonesia and
Morocco. ("What this country needs," Sukarno cried, in one of

his pre-Independence speeches, "is up-to-dateness!" One of Muhammad V's first public acts when he retook his throne was to drive a tractor in a land-improvement ceremony.) And in those circles in industrialized societies concerned with formulating policy toward them it was hardly less so. (Truman's "Point Four" inaugural was but the opening salvo, to be followed by AID, the Peace Corps, the World Bank, and *médecins sans frontiers.*) Peoples who had until recently been "archaic," "tribal," "simple," "subject," "folk," or "primitive" became, quite suddenly, "emergent."

What they were taken to be emerging from was a general condition negatively defined—illiteracy, illness, poverty, passivity, superstition, cruelty, powerlessness. What they were seen as moving toward was equally a general condition, that of the developed world, Europe, the United States, for some the Soviet Union, later on Japan, where these things were, if not absent, markedly reduced. Social advance was fixed, linear, and universal; a path for all places. The Soviets had a particular view of the nature of the end state, the West of the mechanisms involved, the emerging countries of the obstacles in the way, but the underlying image was essentially the same: that, as someone put it, of a freeway with many entrances but only one exit, the one labeled "Modernity."

That, in practice, the matter was less simple, the road less smooth and unidirectional, was a surprise only to enthusiasts—theorists of national liberation, peasant revolution, or economic takeoff into endless growth. What was surprising, and disorganizing as well, was that modernity turned out to be less a fixed destination than a vast and inconstant field of warring possibilities, possibilities neither simultaneously reachable nor systematically connected, neither well defined nor unequivocally attractive. "Becoming modern" was not just closing gaps or negotiating stages, mimicking the West or growing rational. It was laying oneself open to the imaginings of the age and then struggling to realize them. Finding a course, not following one.

The "new nations," "emergent peoples," "LDCs," "Third World states," *pays sur la voie de développement,* some more than others but all to a degree, were projected into a curious situation in which nothing was clear except that something serious had to be done, and quickly, to remodel their character. A good deal of what had to be done was obviously economic. Infrastructure must be laid down, agriculture reformed, industrialism begun, trade encouraged. But it soon became apparent to even the most economistic, the most thoroughly convinced that material progress was but a matter of settled determination, reliable numbers, and proper theory, that political forms, social institutions, religious beliefs, moral practices, even psychological mind-sets would also have to be turned around. Rather a task—obscure, dubious, towering, and disquieting.

It is in the shadow of this task that countries like Indonesia and Morocco, and people from outside, like me, who found themselves absorbed with their fate, and in an odd and derivative way caught up in it, lived during the fifties, sixties, seventies, and eighties, and continue to live today, now that moves toward advance have taken on a gathering force.

It is difficult to convey the texture of this shadow, the yes-and-no, no-and-yes effect it has had on the temper of life in these exigent places. The sense that everything has to be done at once; the sense that if the past can be thrown off and imperialism kept at bay everything is possible. The sense that time is being criminally wasted, opportunities criminally squandered, resources criminally misused; the sense that the world is at last opening up and that one's children and one's children's children will have life chances quite other than those one has had oneself. The sense that change is liberating and that its costs are insupportable; that the common people have at last entered history and that foreign despots have been exchanged for domestic ones; that the thing to do is get out to the West, that the thing to do is dig in and hold on. The sense that it is as dangerous to move as it is to stand stock still.

Relating oneself to so ambiguous and ambivalent a situation—that is, to individuals, mostly ordinary, mostly without much in the way of wealth or power or the promise of such, caught within it—is difficult both morally and practically, especially if one is, given who one is, where one comes from, and what one is about, nothing if not modern, and is, in addition (or perhaps as a result), in some doubt as to whether the order of life current in the West is really the wave of everybody else's future. The co-presence in "developing countries" of so much hope for that future and so much anxiety that it will turn out to be worse than the present (or just an infinite extension of the present), as well as of so much rejection of the past as feudal and oppressive and so much regret for the graces and glories sacrificed in rejecting it, makes it hard for someone himself supposedly "developed," and thus in possession of the life being sought, to know what sort of stance to take toward what is happening either to the society overall or to its individual members.

"Modernity" may not exist as a unitary thing. "Modernization" may mean quite different things when applied to different matters. "Modern life" may not appeal to everyone equally. Yet that does not prevent them, or the idea of them, from setting the terms in which countries like Indonesia and Morocco, thrashing about somewhere between "backward" and "advanced," are these days perceived, discussed, analyzed, and judged, both by the world at large and by their own populations. Certain types of scholars, economists and political scientists especially, tend to have less trouble with this problem than do other sorts, historians, say, or anthropologists, who have the habit of agonizing over it, though there are exceptions on both sides—economists who understand that the infinite messiness of social reality cannot be dismissed as exogenous noise hindering rational progress, anthropologists who are all too ready to instruct whole populations as to how they should arrange their affairs. But there is, in any case, no escaping these slippery categories. Nor, for that matter, the dividedness they cause.

The metaphorical juxtaposition of "modern" and "traditional" images—stolid water buffaloes wallowing in rice terraces with steel and glass skyscrapers rising phantasmally in the distance, burdened camels plodding along at the edge of busy jetports; delicate young women with sarongs and scarves and flowers in their hair running enormous power looms, ominous old men with turbans, jellabas, and wrap-around sunglasses driving BMWs—has become the standard trope for this dividedness. A book entitled *Emerging Indonesia* has on its cover photographs of a sunrise over palm trees, bent women in coolie hats transplanting rice, a wooden bull burning at a Balinese cremation, and a liquid nitrogen plant belching black smoke into a clear, undefiled tropical sky. Another, *Le Maroc aujourd'hui,* pictures in succession the color-drenched dyers' market in the Marrakech medina, a Hollywood swimming pool in a Marrakech hotel garden, a barren mud-house village dwarfed by snow-capped mountains, and an upmarket beach restaurant, terraces, rowboats, and colored umbrellas, in a Berber settlement on the Mediterranean coast.

There is (or was, in 1986) a large shop in the main street of Rabat entirely given over to photographs of the king in every possible style of dress and presentation: praying in the traditional head-to-toe white cloak; riding a horse in jacket and jodhpurs; fishing with rubber boots, creel, and flycaster's hat; posing in military dress, in a cowboy hat, with a polo mallet, in a Western suit and tie; greeting the crowd from an open limousine alongside the pope (himself not unresplendent) in a high-fashion jellaba that looks like damask. A semi-official biography of Suharto pictures him on successive pages standing, a coolie hat on his head, a crude hoe in his hand, in a muddy rice field; on a golf course, in a panama hat and a tee-shirt, swinging a club; seated with his wife at a Balinese ceremony in a sarong and a headscarf, an enormous kris stuck into his belt; greeting the world press, bareheaded in a suit and tie, beside an identically dressed, identically smiling Hubert Humphrey. Hassan II's memoirs begin with two epigraphs: one from the Quran, one from Machiavelli. In the opening chapter of his autobiography (on virtually every other page of which the word "development" occurs), Suharto remarks his reception of an award from the FAO in Rome: "Imagine someone who more than sixty years ago was a child bathing in the mud, leading a peasant's life in a [remote] village, stepping up to the podium and delivering a speech in front of assembled world experts . . ."

Imagine. Everywhere one looks, the traditional-modern, modern-traditional iconography, the neither-nor, both-and imagery of a past half gone and a future half arrived, is taken to sum up the present condition of things, to evoke actuality as it now actually is—which, in fact, clichéd or not, it does very well. The tension between what, writing about this actuality and condition of things, I once called "essentialism" and "epochalism," looking to "The Indigenous Way of Life" (cremations and prayer cloaks, rice paddies and craft markets) as against looking to "The Spirit of the Age" (nitrogen plants and jetports, skyscrapers and golf courses) for self-definition, is so pervasive in Indonesia and Morocco, and, so far as I can see, in a great many other countries, not all of them in Asia and Africa, as to color virtually every aspect of their public life. There may be consensus on the need for modernity; there is only incertitude about the shapes it is taking.

❧

"The Spirit of the Age" is, of course, a difficult thing to define, quite possibly because it doesn't exist or, more likely, because it too much exists in too many expressions. In material matters we at least think we know what it means—joining the ranks of the industrial powers, getting rich, getting healthier, getting skilled, getting armed. Indonesia, which everyone seems to regard as being on the verge of becoming the next Asian dragon, is perhaps a bit further along in this than Morocco, though the difference is not great and Morocco's progress is less noted only because its scale is less grand. But in politics, in art, in religion, in social life, those intricate and changeful practices upon which material matters obscurely depend, we are far less certain as to which way is forward.

In these realms (usually called "cultural," as though science, technology, and economics were not), the hope for gain is shadowed everywhere by the fear of loss. Secularism, commodification, corruption, selfishness, immorality, rootlessness, general estrangement from the sources of value, all the ills attributed to the modern form of life as it has taken shape in the West (and especially, everyone's hard case, in the United States), loom, or seem to, as imminent threats, and the risk of havoc looks at least as real as the promise of ease. It is not just the fact that progress, or its absence, is harder to measure than it is in matters where ICORs, Gini coefficients, GDP, and per capita income can at least be notionally calculated; it is that it is quite unclear how you might calculate (though there are always those who will try) such matters as political openness or oppressiveness, social vitality or enervation, aesthetic power or emptiness, spiritual depth or superficiality. You only know (if then) what these are when you are faced with specific examples of them, concrete and actual—examples such as surprising religious vaudeville in a backwoods Indonesian madrasah, or curious architectural politics in a sorely beset Moroccan medina.

A "madrasah," from the Arabic *darasa*, "to learn," "to study," is, in Indonesia in any case, a religious (that is, Islamic) school organized along Western, classroom lines. It contrasts thus both with the "pesantren," the traditionalist, loose-limbed mosque-school I described in connection with my Acehnese adventure, and with the fully secular, highly regulated state school, the "sekolah," in which by now virtually everyone is enrolled, at least for a few years. It may be anything from a simple primary school to an advanced secondary, or even, increasingly, a tertiary or technically specialized one, so long as it combines a significant amount of both secular and religious instruction in an ordered and graded curriculum. As such, it has always been the leading edge of what has been variously called Muslim reformism, modernism, progressivism, recovery, renaissance, or renewal. Much has changed over the last forty years, both in the form and the content of the institution, and in its role in Indonesian society, but that has not. The madrasah is still the place where the language of Islam engages most immediately the counter-languages of the contemporary world.

The counter-language in this case was quite literally, and, as we shall see, quite figuratively, English. In 1983, three years before I myself became involved with it, a madrasah was founded a few miles from Pare in a rural hamlet called Singgahan—a community, a couple hundred people or so, long noted for the intensity of its piety and, within that piety, for the strength and unanimity of its modernist-reformist, "scripturalist," leanings. (It was to Singgahan that some of the "Communists" I reported earlier as having confessed to planning an attack on the town during the 1965 upheavals were, apparently, delivered for graveside execution.) The founder of the madrasah, one Mhd. Kalend, was not a native of the hamlet. Indeed, he was not even Javanese, but Kalimantanese (that is, Bornean). He had worked as a roustabout in the timber fields there until he saved up enough money to journey to Java and enroll in what is, or anyway was then, the most famous and most innovative modernist madrasah in Indonesia, a place called Gontor, near Madiun in south central Java. After five or six years of study there, he exhausted his resources and set off toward the Pare area, a hundred kilometers to the east, in search of a modernist scholar he had heard was exceptional, a man named Mhd. Yazid, with the idea of apprenticing himself to him.

Yazid was, it so happened, a particularly close friend of mine— what we used, before the term made us nervous, to call a key informant—from my very earliest days in Pare. (Afterward, as foreign embassies got interested in Muslim intellectuals, he traveled to India, the Middle East, and the United States.) Following in the footsteps of his father, also a revered scholar and something of a figure in the Islamist wing of anticolonial nationalist politics, who had died when Yazid was still a child, he ran a small, informal, hushed and bucolic mosque school—a *pesantren*—in his family compound. The compound was located at the farther edge of the village in which, in the fifties, I had lived, where it abutted on Singgahan, the entire population of which Yazid seemed to be related to in one fashion or another. When Kalend, in turn, arrived, well after I had left, seeking a different sort of knowledge, or a different sort of relation to knowledge, from what I had been after, Yazid took him, too, under his wing, and in a short time he was part of this tight little religio-political kinship network.

Kalend married the daughter of the hamlet chief, Yazid's grand-niece. He set up a madrasah in his new father-in-law's administrative compound, a small complex of offices and meeting sheds, using for the purpose his father-in-law's money and contributions from various other local worthies. He enlisted Yazid and his students to supervise the religious side of things. And he installed the intensive study of English as the secular side.

The latter was based (he himself knew virtually no English, and not, as a matter of fact, that much Javanese) on a prefabricated, by-the-numbers instruction program, "The Basic English Course," manufactured in the United States and distributed free by one or another arm of our assistance establishment. He hired English instructors from the state school system to moonlight for him, which, given the inadequacy of their government salaries, they were more than happy to do, and he soon had a student body of about eighty, half and half men and women, from all over the eastern parts of Java. They paid five dollars a month, a serious sum for people who had to work at commercial and day-labor jobs, or beg money from home, in order to subsist. (Most of the courses were held in the late afternoon or early evening, or on weekends.) And what is more, at least a fair proportion learned a decent amount of English, and a few learned a good deal. It's a bit harder for me to judge the effectiveness of the religious side of things. But Yazid was more than a good scholar and a skillful teacher, he was a spiritual presence. As from the first day I met him, the atmosphere around him breathed of a quiet and rigorous reflective faith.

On Idul Fitri (*'īd al-fiṭr*) of 1986, the great holiday that marks the end of the Muslim fast month, the madrasah held its third annual "graduation ceremony" for those fifteen or twenty people who had successfully completed the English course. It took place on the little campus in the hamlet chief's front yard, with perhaps three or four hundred people in attendance—relatives of the graduates, friends of the school, supporters from the local community. Judging from their dress (the women heavily shawled, the men in black jacket, white shirt, and black overseas cap), virtually all of them were members of the more intensely observant, more self-consciously Muslim sector of a society religiously much less singly focused than it has sometimes been represented as being.

This audience, including me, front and center between Yazid and Kalend, sat on folding chairs, facing a small, improvised wooden stage, dimly lit by a generator, and decorated with coconut fronds as for a wedding, a birth, a circumcision, or a shadow-play. To one side of the stage stood a podium equipped with a battery-driven microphone, from which two girls from the school, referred to (in English) as "The Protocol," announced and regulated the evening's program, the first speaking in English, the second immediately following in Indonesian. An expensive-looking, bright-red banner, lettered in silver, of the sort one sees almost exclusively in cities and towns, usually for some governmental occasion or other, was strung across the back of the stage proclaiming, in English, that this was "The Third Reunion of Ex-Students of the Basic English Course, of Singgahan, Pelem," though, unfortunately, "reunion" was misspelled. On the other side of the stage from "The Protocol," a cassette system amplifier, also battery driven, had been set up, from which American popular music blasted at ear-destroying levels whenever the course of things on the stage showed signs of lagging. Even before it started, the event—coconut fronds, folding chairs, Muslim dress, "The Protocol," rock-and-roll, the religious high holiday, and an imperfect, urban-type banner—had a definitely contestatory, multicultural feel about it. Homemade post-modernism, designed to unsettle.

The ceremony (if that is what an off-the-wall production, put together as it went along, should be called) lasted more than five hours, eight in the evening to past one in the morning. The opening phases were purely religious. There was a prayer in Arabic, led by the head of the district office staff in Pare, the only public official in attendance, and he a bit worried to be there. This was followed by a collective recitation of the *fātiha,* the preamble to the Quran, which functions in Islam rather as the Lord's Prayer does in Christianity—the one liturgical form everyone knows. Next came three chantings, elaborate and artful, of a very long quranic passage, first in Arabic by a heavily shawled, virtually veiled, girl, then in Indonesian by a boy in the standard black cap and trousers, and then in English by another boy, similarly dressed, but with white tennis shoes and a garish tie. Three welcoming addresses, also religious in content, by a representative of the graduating class and of each of the two classes already graduated, again one in Arabic, one in Indonesian, and one in English, with the appropriate dress and speech styles, concluded this stage of things. The student performances now began, and the familiarity of established practice, already a bit bent, suddenly, thoroughly, and spectacularly crumbled.

Three quite small boys, no more than seven or eight years old, appeared as if from nowhere. They were mimes, made up in whiteface but otherwise uncostumed in their sleeveless half-shirts and their short pants, dead silent and without expression. In excruciating slow motion, that seemed to defy the law of gravity, they proceeded to conduct a mock street brawl, entirely in gestures. They kneed one another, goosed one another, tripped one another up, knocked one another over, booted one another in the behind, slapped one another's face, snatched at one another's genitals, socked one another in the nose or eye, in no apparent pattern, and then they collapsed, after ten minutes or so, into a heap in the center of the stage, so many rag dolls. Or perhaps so many exhausted balloons. For a fourth boy then came on and gradually, body section by body section, mime-pumped them back up again, after which they left the stage as precipitously as they had come, unfurling from somewhere a black banner that read "Happy Idul Fitri!"

The point of all this was obscure, not just to me, but to the audience in general. People whispered hypotheses and counter-hypotheses to one another, as they did with rising urgency during the entire evening, as to what the devil was going on. About all I could make of it, save that perhaps someone had seen a Three Stooges movie, was that it was some sort of mute salute, impudent and ironical, to the speaking—or rather the non- or not-yet speaking—of English, a supposition immediately confirmed when the next act, this one at least announced, came on: six or seven young men, of perhaps nineteen or twenty, also mimes, even more spectacularly talented, who called themselves, in English, "The Street Boys."

The performance of this group went on for more than an hour. The central figure was a man in whiteface and mirror glasses, who was dressed in a hyper-urban, Jakarta-hustler style—slouch hat, broad-lapel day-glo suit, two-toned shoes, obvious wrist watch, impossible tie. He entered pulling on an imaginary rope, dragging the others of the troupe out of the shadows one by one. Each of these moved in a different manner—a jerking mechanical man, a strutting pimp, a prancing madman, a flapping rag doll, someone who may have been supposed to have been gay. Once they were on stage, their mouths were opened automatically, one by one, by a startle clap from the central figure, who put lighted cigarettes in them. He then caused them, with another startle clap, to hold the cigarettes at arms' length, and then, turning his back on them, left them frozen in various eccentric poses for several minutes, during which he, still silently, mocked and taunted them, trying to disturb their impassivity. Finally, he tied them all up into a single bundle, insulting them as he did so with various sorts of obscene pokings and grabbings, at which point they all burst suddenly into song, in English:

> I went to the theater
> It was very interesting
> But I didn't enjoy it
> People were in front of me
> People were in back of me
> I got very angry.

They sang this ditty over and over again in a series of over-the-top parodies of popular song styles: the Indonesian ones called *dangdut* and *kroncong,* Bob Dylan, hard rock, country, what may have been Elvis, and a number of others I didn't certainly recognize. Finished with that, they closed with a mime of a student attempting, with wild desperation and high unsuccess, to learn English from a book, and departed to the sounds of bewildered muttering and confused applause.

If the audience, now grown extremely uneasy indeed, was not sufficiently put off by this, an even more extraordinary event, considering who we (a couple of Chinese and me excepted) were and what we were celebrating, now took place.

It began, innocently enough, with a very bad guitar solo by the son of the man from the district office who had given the benediction and an exceedingly lachrymose poem in English, "Message to My Mother," declaimed in a dramatically agonized tone by a young girl ("Don't worry / I love you"), who had apparently written it. But immediately this, whatever it was, was completed, three young women—I would guess they were sixteen or seventeen—burst noisily onto the stage dressed in extremely garish, wildly clashing, mod-singer clothes. They wore very short skirts, very heavy makeup, great cascades of costume jewelry, and, again, dark glasses; and their brassieres were stuffed to overflowing. They were so outlandish that I thought at first that they were cross-dressed men. These mimic-whores performed (in English, though not very intelligible English) a rock-song parody, accompanied with bump and grind movements, leers, skirt-swishings, and yeh-yeh cries. This was surely the most subversive performance in a fairly subversive evening, and the audience, including Yazid, Kalend, and me, watched in stunned and wide-eyed silence. When I asked them what this was all about, I got a thin smile from the one and a murderous stare from the other.

After these apparitions departed, the tension only rose, for there now leapt onto the stage, I think unscheduled, and certainly unprepared for, a young man dressed as a student and carrying a bright yellow folder. He began racing erratically about as maniacs do, seeing imaginary things, snatching at empty air, rambling inconsequently on in gibberish English. He studied the folder with exaggerated attention, grimaced, tore out the pages and threw them about, uttered strange sounds and adopted strange positions, until it became clear that he was not just "acting crazy," he was the real thing. A number of students and teachers, even a couple of people from the audience, came on to the stage to try to talk him—in Indonesian—into leaving, but he angrily resisted. The collective anxiety which had been building through the night threatened now to get a bit out of hand; people were beginning to shout, frightened, from the crowd. But after a while, a long while, the man finally subsided and allowed himself to be led off, limp and disconsolate, but still spouting in meaningless English, into the dark, and things calmed down a bit.

The final phases of the festivities (it was now after midnight) both put matters more or less back on track and re-introduced something recognizably Islamic into the proceedings. Yazid gave an elegant sermon in excellent English. (It was the first time I had ever heard him speak it. We conversed largely in Indonesian, now and then in Javanese; only formulaically in Arabic.) Starting off with the Quranic sura, "All men know We have created you from a male and female and have made you nations and tribes that you may know one another," and the hadith about seeking knowledge even unto China, he urged tolerance between religion and religion, nation and nation, color and color, language and language.

After I gave a brief, impromptu address, first in English, then in Indonesian, expressing my gratitude for being there, my hopes for the future success of the madrasah, and so on (my wife, an American Indianist who does not speak Indonesian, also was hauled up for a few words, which I then translated), Kalend closed the evening with a very long, very fiery sermon in political Indonesian, ambiguously referent to the significance of what we had just seen:

> You should not think that if you know English you will become modern and forget the norms and ideals of Islam and can transcend established religion. The purpose of studying English is to serve Allah, not to advance one's personal fortunes. English is a "seed" for Islam and it is not to be used to undermine Islam. I am not afraid of the West! I welcome the West! But I *am* afraid of losing true religious feeling!

After this, delivered in an angry shout for nearly an hour, and a final prayer in Arabic, "The Protocol"—"Good Night" . . . "Slamet Malem"—closed the proceedings, and we shuffled away, mumbling.

"The Meaning" of all this, just what was being said, and unsaid, by whom, to whom, with what purpose, in this parade of trans-

gressions bracketed with ritualisms, from Marceau's Bip, through
Ionesco's "Language Lesson," to Lucky's speech in *Godot,* is fairly
well obscure. (It is very doubtful that any of the participants had
even heard of, much less witnessed any of these, with the possible
exception of Marceau, or Marceau imitators—that rope is too
reminiscent—on television, and maybe, as I suggested, the Three
Stooges, whom Siberian hunters and African pygmies have seen
by now.)

But, even though no one, participants or onlookers, seemed
willing to discuss the affair, about which they appeared to be either
embarrassed or angry, it seems clear on the face of things that a
tension between a desire to make connection with life at its most
contemporary and a determination to maintain the essential im-
pulses of a severe, puritanical Islam, deeply rooted in local emotions, animated the whole occasion. The evening was a stream of
moralities, mockeries, ambivalences, ironies, outrages, and contradictions, almost all of them centering in one way or another around
language and the speaking (half-speaking, non-speaking) of language. Uncrossable lines were crossed in play, irrationalities were
displayed in heavy quotation marks, codes were mixed, rhetorics
were apposed, and the whole project to which the school was
dedicated, extending the impact of Islam, perhaps the most lin-
guistically self-conscious of the great religions, on the world
through the learning of a world language, was put into question.
(This was the only public performance in Pare I have ever witnessed where Javanese played absolutely no role at all, save, of
course, among the whispering auditors trying to organize their
confusions and contain their outrages, hardly any of whom, as a
final irony, knew any English at all.)

Whatever else was accomplished, the stammerings of religious
modernity, for that matter of modernity in general, were most
eloquently articulated. The aporias of discourse—"qua, qua,
qua"—are everywhere now.

What body movement is to kinesthetical Java, absorbed in dance,
gesture, posture, and politesse, the look of the built environment—
cities, buildings, spaces, rooms, and the furnishings of rooms—is

to architectural Morocco, absorbed in ornament, texture, design, and decor. The shapes of the physical setting within which life takes form, gates and walls, fountains and carpets, divans and minarets, tiled floors and calligraphic signboards, articulate that life, lend to it a hard and visible moral surface. Playing with it, like playing with the choreographical grammar of Java, produces, therefore, more serious sorts of expression than might at first appear.

In late February of 1986, a week or two before the massive joint celebration of the twenty-fifth anniversary of Hassan II's accession to the Moroccan throne and the tenth of his launching of the Green March into the Sahara (the March actually took place in November of 1975, but it was ritually assimilated to Coronation Day for this milestone occasion), the recently elected municipal council of Sefrou issued, with neither warning nor explanation, a most curious decree. Henceforth, the color of all buildings in the town was to be beige, *crème* in the French redaction, *qehwi* in the in the Arabic: paint could be obtained at designated outlets. Compliance with the decree was, as one would expect, very far from complete, and the town remained in fact more white than anything else, and when not white, pastel. But, as one would not expect (at least I did not), the decree was, among certain sorts of people in certain sections of the town, immediately and completely obeyed. Brightly colored, variegated house facades, some of them masterpieces of design bravura, were painted over during the course of the day into a dun homogeneity.

Behind this event, trivial in itself and of very uncertain permanency of effect, lay a long and far from trivial story. The changing shape of the town, its changing social composition, the changing relations between it and its hinterland, its economic base, its governing elites, and the national power, and, most critical of all, the changing sense on the part of its inhabitants as to what *citadinité* (that French word that translates so awkwardly into English but so readily, as *mudaniyya*, "belonging *to* and *in* a city, a *medīna*," into Arabic) really means, were all caught up in a bitter and many-sided debate—a debate about what a proper Islamic city, "a place of 'religion' *(dīn),*" ought these days to be, how it ought to feel, what it ought to look like.

There has been in recent years, just as the thing itself seems finally to be yielding to grids, roundabouts, shop windows, monuments, and grand boulevards, a great deal of discussion in scholarly circles, mostly but not entirely Western, concerning this whole notion of "The Islamic City." Is there such a thing? If there is such a thing, can we say what is Islamic about it? If there is such a thing and we can say what is Islamic about it, does its religious character matter to its practical functioning? The exaggeration of the uniformity of city life in the Islamic world, the idealized quality of descriptions of that life, the tendency to see such cities against the background of European experiences, and a stereotyped, ahistorical concept of "Islam" as a social force within them have all come in for severe attack. The very idea now comes with a question mark welded onto it.

There is, of course, much to be said for these queries and criticisms, though perhaps not as much as has been said. Surely, there has been a good deal of constructing of chimeras, imagined entities that never were, in scholarly work on North African and Middle Eastern cities. But, just as surely, there has been a good deal of genuine discovery in such work that ought not to be discarded simply because it proceeded from an outlook, the despised "orientalism" of textualist scholars, not now in favor. In any case, whatever the status of the idea of The Islamic City is in scholarly discourse, it is very much alive in the minds of many workaday Muslims. In fact, it is made even more alive by the enormous transformations cities and towns are now undergoing throughout the Islamic world. "A certain idea of a city" becomes more vivid and more absorbing as it becomes harder to see it in the sprawl of modern urban life, grows increasingly significant as a dream and a memory as the conditions of its existence decay and disappear.

There is, by now, hardly a city or town in the whole of the Middle East, however ancient, that presents an historically coherent face to the world. This is, of course, true to some extent throughout Asia and Africa, and few Western cities even pretend any longer to an abiding identity. But it seems especially characteristic of Arabo-Islamic cities, and certainly of Moroccan ones, certainly of Sefrou, because new city forms tend less to replace old ones, to update them, or to swallow them up, than to grow up around them, leaving the old ones more or less intact. "Old Medinas," "New Medinas," "New Cities," "Spontaneous . . . Clandestine . . . Peripheral . . . Habitations," are all in place at once, like remains from different floors of a successively occupied archaeological site spread out horizontally for comparative inspection. The urban landscape is not merely various, as are all such landscapes—it is disjunct, a set of settings. It is within such a landscape of different orderings, growing out of different forms of life, and pointing in different directions, that the public argument about The Islamic City, an argument of buildings and institutions, facades and ideologies, street nets and public services, takes place.

In the history of Sefrou, and most emphatically in its recent history, as I have briefly recounted it earlier on, all these matters come together: the disarticulation of the urban landscape; the concern with the idea of The Islamic City as a permanent norm; the difficulty of defining such an idea in the context of the disarticulation; the sense that the idea, and with it Islam itself, is endangered; the "reading-in" (or, to adapt a phrase of Richard Wollheim's, the "seeing-in") of all this into the changing physical appearance of the city. Like graduation-day pantomimes, governmental efforts to control the color of houses are passing happenings. But, in settings where ornament, design, and the particularity of spaces have a special salience, they, too, catch up a lot of themes.

On the eve of the Protectorate, in 1911, the city (or town: there is no distinction in Arabic) of Sefrou was ten hectares in size, contained six thousand people, and consisted of the walled old city of passages and impasses, the *madīna qadīma;* an impacted Jewish quarter, the *mellaḥ,* in the dead center of it; and a small citadel, also walled, the *qalʿa,* just above it. A decade later, in 1922, with the Protectorate firmly in place and the city officially municipalized, it was thirteen times as large, a hundred and thirty hectares, and consisted of the old areas plus a new Arab quarter, laid out on a gridiron plan just outside the walls, and a French suburb, gardens, *maisons,* and curving streets, in the hills above the citadel. In 1944, toward the close of the Protectorate, the municipal boundaries were expanded again, to three hundred and eighty hectares (the population now was approaching twenty thousand), the added areas being more "new medina" quarters plus some neo-Moorish civic spaces. And there the borders stayed until 1982, when a Socialist municipal government, recently and almost accidently come to power and facing, with most uncertain prospects, its first reelection campaign, suddenly, amid intense controversy, some of it violent, more than tripled the city's official size, to twelve hundred hectares, so as to bring within its political orbit the "spontaneous," "clandestine," "peripheral" settlements that had sprung up with stunning rapidity during the previous decade, and whose votes the Socialists saw as theirs. This was a revolution (or an attempt at such, for in the event it failed) through municipal redefinition.

The cultural genealogy of the city can be seen unfolding in this stage-by-stage augmentation of it to a hundred and twenty times its original extent (and nine times its population) over the course of seventy years. One after another, intrusive forms of life, French, Franco-Moroccan, Country Moroccan (mostly Berber in speech and pastoralist in culture), come to take up one or another part of its site, distributing themselves around its Arab and Judeo-Arab medina core, which in turn is locked in place, a crumbling relic. Some of these forms of life—the French, the Jewish—have, as mentioned earlier, largely disappeared to Marseilles and Jerusalem. But after the Socialists came to power in 1976 (and especially after they attempted to stay in power by incorporating the settlement areas into the body of the city seven years later) the distinction between what I earlier called, as they do themselves, "old" or "real" or "genuine" Sefrouis, descendants of families resident there (or so they claim) for hundreds of years, and "new" or "outsider" or "alien" Sefrouis, recently gathered around its edges, became the main axis of social, economic, and political conflict. "The city used to eat the countryside," an old inhabitant said bleakly to me. "Now the countryside eats the city."

The "old" ("real" . . . "genuine" . . .) Sefrouis are, for the most part, merchants, professionals, landholders, or civil servants—sometimes all of these at once; and although they come in all classes, from the abject poor to the crocodile rich, the unusually compact city elite (a tight little clique whose members are few enough to be listable), is drawn, as it apparently always has been, from among them. Perhaps a third of the Muslim, Jewish, and French population at the time of Independence, they make up today perhaps a third of the (larger) City Muslim-Country Muslim one. Most of them now live outside the old city core. The middling classes—smaller shopkeepers, minor clerks, repairmen, and the like—have been moving since the nineteen forties into the "new medina" gridiron quarters just outside the walls, which were built expressly to accommodate them, leaving only the poor (and the traditional bazaars) behind. The elite, anchored as it was in se-cluded family alleyways, private neighborhoods gated off from the noise of the world, was slower to abandon the old medina; but since the late sixties virtually all of its members, the bulk of whom belong to seven or eight large local families, have by now moved into the suburban houses vacated by the departed French. They have also inherited, from the same French, the municipal admini-stration, strengthened their economic position, and related them-selves to the monarchy as "king's men," much as their fathers had related themselves to the Protectorate government as *notables indigènes*. During the independence struggle itself, their grip was briefly shaken by the power of upstart nationalist leaders, mostly from the Muslim reformist party, Istiqlal; but it was soon restored as the monarchy, reasserting its own ascendancy, reasserted theirs. By the time of the 1963 municipal elections, they were back in place—the same men, with the same interests, the same resources, and the same understanding of mudaniyya: Arabo-Islamic "city-hood."

The "new" ("outsider" . . . "alien" . . .) Sefrouis, who flooded in during the seventies and eighties and still are coming, settled,

as mentioned, along the edges of the already expanded new medina, in areas either previously unoccupied because stony or pre-
cipitous or, increasingly, and to the old Sefrouis more disturbingly,
in the *huerta* (Spanish for "orchard")—the irrigated olive groves
that, forming the city's aesthetic frame and providing a fair amount
of its income, have been for centuries the sign of its "oasis" felicity.
Nor did they install themselves, as rural migrants so often have in
the great conurbations along the coast—Casablanca, Rabat-Salé,
Tangiers, Safi—in shabby and impermanent *bidonvilles*, "tin can"
slums of shacks and lean-tos. Supported by returns from recently
sold-off farms and, more important, by remittances from relatives
working in Europe, they built, or had built for them, solid, plas-
tered stone, city-like houses, sizeable structures, designed to be
noticed and to last. Their arrival in the city changed, therefore,
more than its social complexion. It changed, as earlier intrusions
had not (or only marginally), its aspect, air, demeanor, look. What
was once a "chiseled jewel" in "a paradisian garden" was now a
sprawling, disorganized, anything but jewel-like *bourg*—a sour
French word everyone in the city seems somehow now to know.

This transformation of the city from an urban solidity in a tribal
flux to a tumble of buildings, people, and institutions, was bound
to issue eventually in political expression, even in a traditionalist
monarchy generally resistant to popular politics. When the ratio
of urban to rural population radically changes, when city property
values skyrocket, when a majority of the houses are without running water, sewers, electricity, or effective road access, and when
large amounts of funds from foreign remittances are flowing into
an economy in which the proportion of people without work
("those," as the idiom has it, "who stand against the wall") is
increasing by leaps and bounds, the established power structure,
no matter how long it has been in place, no matter how closely
knit it is, and no matter how firmly it is reinforced by central
authority, is going to be put under something of a strain.

The extent of this strain became suddenly apparent in the municipal council elections of 1976, when that structure, in fact,
cracked. The representatives of the traditional elite, who had mo-

nopolized the council since Lyautey set it up in 1913, were sum-
marily turned out, and the Moroccan Socialist party, never before
much of a factor, won, to everyone's astonishment, including its
own, three-quarters of the seats. Though the council, hemmed in
on all sides by bureaucratic and police control in a system euphem-
istically called "tutelage," is quite limited in its capacity to act on
its own, it is, simply by virtue of being the only popularly elected
body of any importance in a local government otherwise centrally
appointed, the main expression of locally rooted power balances.
The dramatic displacement from it of the sons and grandsons of
the men who traditionally manned it, a public humiliation of great
consequence, inaugurated a kind of Prague Spring in Sefrou: a
period, seven years as a matter of fact, in which an unexpectedly
opened door was, amid rising tension, strong outside pressure, and
a significant amount of hands-on violence, relentlessly and, so it
seems, definitively, re-shut.

This odd interregnum, a populist moment in a paternalist system, was made possible by the monarchy's practice, inherited from
the Protectorate and further perfected, of using municipal elections as a form of public-opinion polling. Elections are, in general,
carefully controlled, but at each one, certain localities are allowed
a relatively free rein in order to bring political realities into open
view. How does the land lie? Who must be dealt with? The next
time, this strategical freedom disappears and other localities get a
chance to have a less fettered vote. In 1976 it was Sefrou's turn to
experience opinion polling democracy; in 1983, a term expired,
the experiment was over. The old Sefroui elite was thrust bodily
back into office. Not a single Socialist was returned, the party
collapsed as a local force, its main leaders, fearing arrest or worse,
left the city.

But, however brief, the Socialist interlude brought the question
of what sort of city Sefrou ought properly to be into heightened
relief. The displacement of the old Sefroui elite, the extension of
the city's boundaries, and thus of voting rights and the claim to
city services, to include the new Sefroui settlements, and the
vigorous attempt on the part of the council to increase its freedom

of action vis-à-vis the central administrative apparatus—to weaken "tutelage"—challenged not only traditional privileges and traditional exclusions. It challenged also the idea of the Islamic City within whose frame such privileges and exclusions were defined. Setting out to make a local social revolution, an enterprise in which they largely failed and were, in the nature of the case, doomed to fail, the Socialists made, more or less inadvertently (as they, too, were traditionalists so far as their tastes were concerned), at least the beginnings of a cultural one. They left the material economy about as they found it. They left the symbolic economy, the figuration of city space, thoroughly transformed.

What the Socialist interruption interrupted was not the directions of change that had, well before its advent, gripped the city, and which continued to advance after it was over. It interrupted the way in which those directions were represented, perceived, and understood. By enfranchising the new Sefroui population, not just in legal terms, which, in a traditional "tutelage" state, do not matter all that much, but in moral terms, which, in such a state, especially if it is Muslim, matter a very great deal, the Socialists reinforced the new Sefrouis' determination to be included within the body of the city, to be inscribed in its landscape. But it also reinforced, and at least as powerfully, the old Sefrouis' determination to set the criteria, lifestyle criteria on the one hand, attitudinal criteria on the other, upon which such inclusion and inscription properly rest. The clash of those determinations—what are the signs of mudaniyya now?—came to be, and have remained, at the very center of social struggle.

Shortly before the double celebration I mentioned of his quarter-century as king and his decade as Saharan commander, Hassan II gave a speech in his new palace at Marrakech—broadcast on the state radio and television—to the association of Moroccan architects and city planners, "a veritable course on architecture and urbanism," as the royalist newspaper *Le Matin du Sahara* had it.

Morocco has been marked at each great period in its history, His Majesty said, by an architectural originality. One recognizes immediately the monuments and buildings of the Idrisi, Al-moravid, Almohad, Sa'adi, and 'Alawi periods. Each dynasty has stamped its epoch with its style. (The first of these dynasties is semi-mythical; it dates from the eighth century and is supposedly the period when Islam arrived and Fez was founded. The last is Hassan's own, which arose in the seventeenth century.) Now, however, a decline has set in. All sorts of ill-designed and ill-constructed buildings are appearing haphazardly around the edges of our ancient cities. Garish European-style houses, vulgar and ostentatious, are proliferating in the wealthy quarters. The classic form of the Moroccan Islamic city, the flower of our cultural greatness, is disappearing into a nondescript, alien sprawl.

For example, he said, take Sefrou. Not long ago it was a lovely little place, with its gardens, its walls, its mosques, nestled at the foot of the Middle Atlas—a beautiful expression (he called it a jewel) of the authentic Moroccan tradition. Now it had become shapeless and ugly (*laide,* though he was speaking Arabic). Faced with the prospect of a doubling of our housing capacity by the year 2000, it is necessary to construct "Moroccan for the Moroccans [*sic,* in English]." We must give to our works a national character. We must preserve, amid modernization, that which is beautiful and authentic, conserve (as apparently Sefrou has not) the spiritual identity, Muslim and Maghrebian at the same time, of Moroccan architecture and urban form. As the *Le Matin* report concludes, in case anyone has managed to miss the point: "One understands from this that His Majesty, Hassan II, whose reign is one of the most glorious and most productive of our History, wishes to leave his mark, as brilliantly as he has politically and economically, through an original architecture, modern and authentically Moroccan, in a word through an architecture."

The king's little "course," singling out Sefrou before the entire country as an egregious case of un-Moroccan, un-Islamic urban blight, shook, as might be imagined, the recently reinstalled old Sefroui city council quite severely, especially as it was followed almost immediately by an official reprimand and a command from the provincial governor at Fez to "do something" by Accession Day. But, in fact, it merely brought to a boil a process of cultural confrontation already well under way in the city.

The dismay of the old Sefrouis over the city's physical transformation had grown to enormous proportions during the Socialist period, producing a litany of moral complaint, class resentment, and aesthetic nostalgia, thick enough to cut with a knife. And it also brought with it the beginnings of a self-conscious effort to recreate the institutions, and the look, of a proper Islamic City.

The traditional office of *muḥtasib,* a combination religious preceptor, moral policeman, and market administrator, once extremely powerful but fallen into almost complete disuse, was restored to political prominence in 1982 during the bitter struggle that returned the old guard to power. A long-time traditional leader (and, as an Alawi sherif, a distant relative of the king) was appointed to it, and he promptly indicted the Socialists as "atheists." An extremely large, classically styled mosque, built by the state and called the Hassan II, was completed just outside the walls, replacing the old grand mosque in the medina (which was itself refurbished) as the official city mosque, and the muhtasib was designated as its *imām* and *ḵaṭīb,* prayer leader and Friday sermon giver. Other classically Muslim offices—the *nīẓir,* administrator of religious properties; the *qāḍī,* religious judge; the *'ādel,* notary; the *muqqadem,* quarter chief; the *amīn,* craft guild head— were similarly reemphasized as canonical features of a genuinely Islamic city. Public baths, public ovens, neighborhood prayer houses, market fountains, and other traditional civic institutions were renovated, and there was an outburst of demonstrative private mosque building by leading notables, anxious to express their piety, their solidity, and their continued importance.

At the same time as this cultural, or religio-cultural, revivalism (a fair amount of which was essentially cosmetic) was developing on the old Sefroui side, a counter-assertion, in a vocabulary at once similar and rather different, was taking place on the new Sefroui side. Fed at once by the Socialists' courtship of them, by their rapidly swelling numbers, and by their sense of being, nonetheless, treated as barbarian intruders, morally unwelcome and materially neglected, the new Sefrouis' presentation of themselves as authentic city people *(madanī)*, their determination to move from the margins to full inclusion in urban society, grew steadily more intense. (The term the new Sefrouis use to refer to their move from the country to the town is not the old Sefrouis' *exode rural,* another sour French term which makes them sound like tattered refugees, but *hijra,* the Arabic at once for emigration and immigration, and, of course, for that most world-altering migration of all, the Prophet's move from Mecca to Medina that inaugurated the Muslim Era.) And this determination, the determination to complete their hijra, is also most emphatically expressed in an architectural idiom—in a rhetoric of mosques and houses and, most especially, and most surprisingly, of facades.

Facades are surprising, or, perhaps at the level of materialized meaning we are confronted with here, unsurprising, because, as has often been remarked, classical medina houses are turned radically inward. They present to the public streets and alleyways a uniform and (a chastely decorated door occasionally aside) extremely subdued face: whitened walls and small, grilled windows well above eye level. It is in interior courts, gardens, and reception rooms, brocaded women's quarters, mosaic fountains, and carpeted tea salons, that status display takes place. From outside, a rich man's home and a poor one's look hardly different; within, they contrast as a palace to a hovel in their decorations, furnishings, and use of space. Certainly this is true in Sefrou; not only in the old city, the medina proper, where there are virtually no external markings at all and a street looks like a solid wall, irregularly punctured with narrow entryways, but in the immediate extramural, new medina quarters as well, where one does not know (at least if one is a stranger) prior to entry whether one will be confronted by a cave or a jewel box. And it is this, perhaps the most charged domain, certainly the most intimate, of urban imagery that the new Sefrouis in their sprung-up settlements have completely reversed. They have turned the city house, decoratively anyway, inside out.

As mentioned, the houses the new Sefrouis have built are mostly substantial stone and concrete structures, many of them quite large, and they are arranged haphazardly, given their "illegal," thus opportunistic siting, along rutted paths and tracks. Inside, most of them are strikingly bare. Indeed, they are often virtually empty— large spaces with but an isolated bed or a forlorn table and a few chairs. Most of their owners' capital is sunk in the structure itself and the hyperinflated land on which it is built, and the absence of city services, water, electricity, and the like limits in any case what can be done: there are no reflecting pools or back-lit divans here. It is on the exterior walls that display occurs. Almost all these houses are (or, anyway, were, until the edict) very brightly painted in bold, primary colors—reds, yellows, greens, blues, even now and then purples, oranges, and pinks—garishly intermixed. Most were further decorated, usually in an all-over fashion, with intricate designs, some based on traditional craft motifs, taken from carpets, textiles, pottery, and leather work, some traditional magical images (the hand of Fatima, geomantic figures, the name of Allah, or even the whole *fātiha* written out in elaborate calligraphy), some tribal marks, derived from the female face-tatoos that pass among Berber women for the equivalent of the urban veil. Others were simply original inventions, come upon, people said, in dreams or visions.

The common term for these flamboyant facades (which, as they tend to be four-walled, are perhaps more exactly referred to as envelopes) is the French *fantasia,* the term long used for the famous horsemanship and powder-play display of tribal Moroccans—like those displays, they are public demonstrations of individual force. They are, as everyone recognizes, both the new Sefrouis who produce them and the old Sefrouis, who wish to erase them, statements, claims, announcements, arguments, demands. Similarly, the edict that the facades were to be painted over in civilized beige was more than the council's response to "do something" visibly and quickly before Accession Day. It was a move, or rather a countermove, in what had become a quite self-conscious politics of signs.

Turning their houses inside-out, the new Sefrouis threatened to turn Sefrou as a whole inside-out; to make its demonstrative peripheries, not its restrained core, its defining feature. The aesthetic and moral reaction by the old Sefrouis to the facades as offenses against mudaniyya was, if anything, more passionate than their concern with intruders' material claims, which they felt able enough to hold at bay. Where the Socialists had sought to accommodate the in-migrants' demands for inclusion in urban society by legally incorporating them into the municipality, the notables of the council (and the, often more important, notables around the council) sought to make them, now that they were, alas, so included, at least look, and one might hope, behave, like proper urbanites.

The upshot was a bit of a compromise. Most of the new Sefrouis did paint over their houses (the peripheries changed color almost overnight), in exchange for an implicit recognition of them as proper citizens, entitled to proper services, not illegal squatters who ought to be (as the more conservative members of the old elite wished them to be) bulldozed away. But this compromise, if that's the word for it, hardly ended the confrontation. It merely moved it onto a new plane of discussion, one in which the issues are represented as being between various interests within the city, not between it and aliens gathered along its edges. Consider, for example, a remarkable letter in an Arabic-language newspaper, written about two years later by a resident of the city's largest, fastest-growing, and most energetic peripheral settlement:

> One of the most astounding things is the scarcity of drinkable water in Sefrou, though it lies at the foot of the Middle Atlas. This fact is one of the paradoxes that leave the observer in perplexity trying to answer a clamor of questions . . .
>
> Here we reach the subject of this correspondence, which we publish on behalf of the families living in the quarter Bni Seffar, who request, through it, that the big problem of drinkable water be

attended to and that the needs of about 2,500 people be met.

This quarter does not have more than a single fountain, toward which its inhabitants rush early in the morning in order to grasp a few drops of its watery generosity.

We do not speak here of the long line, of the long waiting, of the fights that arise among the waiting people . . .

What the residents are asking for is for the opportunity of benefiting from the drinkable water to be given to all without discrimination, especially as it has been observed that those in charge of the distribution favor certain sides [factions, parties] against others. That is clear from their giving the privilege of obtaining water to some residents and neglecting others.

The residents of the quarter request from the members of their municipal council, who poured promises upon them during the election campaign [against the Socialists], to stop this favoritism and consider all the residents as equals, no difference between this one and that one, but only in light of his acts in the service of the general interest.

What these humble people request is nothing more than the simplest of human rights; just some water to quench their thirst, and they will not upset [alarm, threaten] anyone! They want only water . . .!?

To change the face of a city, or the facade of a house, is, here anyway, to change the way those who live in it see it and understand it, and to put under pressure the cultural assumptions in terms of which they have been used to seeing it, understanding it, and living in it. Auden's famous line "a new style of architecture, a change of heart" is more than a literary conceit. What is happening in Sefrou to the Islamic City, like what is happening in Pare to Islamic education, is what is happening both in those places and elsewhere to "Islam" as such. It is losing definition and gaining energy.

ﻋﺮ

It is difficult to know what to do with the past. You can't live in it, no matter how much you may fantasize doing so, or how gravely nostalgic you grow when remembering it. You can't foretell the future from it, however suggestive, promising, or ominous it may seem; things in the offing frequently don't arrive, things unhinted at frequently do. You can't, in my view anyway, draw laws out of it universally applicable to social affairs, iron necessities determining measurable outcomes, though attempts to do so seem as unending as they are futile. And you can't, or anyway, again, I can't, find eternal verities in it by which to resolve the incertitudes of everyday existence or quiet the paradoxes of public conduct; there are, indeed, no master plots. About the only thing it seems useful for (besides, that is, and perhaps primarily, the sheer appreciation of it as what people have gone through) is perceiving, a bit less blankly, what is happening around one, reacting, a bit more intelligently, to what, in the event, swims into view. Of all the bromides about the past, that it is prologue, that it is a bucket of ashes, that it is another country, that it is not even past, that if you don't remember it you are condemned to repeat it, that it is the debris that piles up in front of us as we back into heaven, about the only one that comes to much as usable truth is Kierkegaard's "Life is lived forward but it is understood backward."

What will become of Pare or Sefrou, Indonesia or Morocco, Anthropology or Islam, of the grand configuration of world wealth and power or of the life chances of local intellectuals trying to reconcile their faith with the way we live now or to reconstruct politics in a less archaic mode, is obscure; waits, as we say, upon events, remains to be seen, is anybody's guess. Yet that, too, the easy complacency of quietist thought, cannot be right. When what is coming, whatever is coming, at length arrives, we surely will describe it (what else, unless we are to self-deconstruct and retreat into attitudes, can we do?) as further chapters in continuing narratives—extensions, connections, clarifications, and reconsiderations of half-told tales, still half-told. The arrows that point off at so many angles, backwards, forwards, sideways, obliquely, in the language comedy of the madrasah graduation or the civic rhetoric of the painting decree, will, in time, sum themselves up into at least something of a direction. We may not be able to trace the track of modernity before it is laid down; but once it is we shall have explanations enough, and not necessarily untrue or unuseful ones, for the course it has taken. There may not be any certain relation between what has happened and what is going to, but whatever pops up we will, bound as we are to sequence and sense, doubtless suggest one, conceivably accurate. You can't read a text before it has been written. You can't do much else (save ignore it or pulverize it) once it has.

There is, tucked away in a footnote in Jerome Bruner's fine little book, *Acts of Meaning*—a predecessor to my own in the Jerusalem-Harvard Lectures series—a reference to an Indian story which makes the point with the compact wit of traditional parable. It is from Kalidasa's *Sakuntala,* "the most famous drama in Sanskrit literature," and was brought to Bruner's attention, in service of a different concern, by an Israeli scholar. A sage is squatted before a real elephant that is standing right in front of him. The sage is saying, "This is *not* an elephant." Only later, as the elephant turns and begins to lumber away, does a doubt begin to arise in the sage's mind about whether there might not be an elephant around after all. Finally, when the elephant has altogether disappeared from view, the sage looks down at the footprints the beast has left behind and declares with certainty, "An elephant *was* here."

For me at least (and that is the "we" we are talking about here), anthropology, ethnographical anthropology, is like that: trying to reconstruct elusive, rather ethereal, and by now wholly departed elephants from the footprints they have left on my mind. "After the fact," is a double pun, two tropological turns on a literal meaning. On the literal level, it means looking for facts, which I have, of course, "in fact" been doing. On the first turning, it means ex-post interpretation, the main way (perhaps the only way) one can come to terms with the sorts of lived-forward, understood-backward phenomena anthropologists are condemned to deal with. On the second (and even more problematical) turning, it means the post-positivist critique of empirical realism, the move away from simple correspondence theories of truth and knowledge which makes of the very term "fact" a delicate matter. There is not much assurance or sense of closure, not even much of a sense of knowing what it is one precisely *is* after, in so indefinite a quest, amid such various people, over such a diversity of times. But it is an excellent way, interesting, dismaying, useful, and amusing, to expend a life.

Notes

Index

Notes

Notes are keyed by page number.

1. Towns

4. "Pare in the early fifties": The original study of Pare was, as explained below, a group project. The main publications on the town emerging from this work include: A. G. Dewey, *Peasant Marketing in Java* (New York, 1962); D. R. Fagg, "Authority and Social Structure: A Study in Javanese Bureaucracy" (Ph.D. diss., Harvard University, 1958); C. Geertz, *The Religion of Java* (Glencoe, Ill., 1960); C. Geertz, *Peddlers and Princes* (Chicago, 1963); C. Geertz, *The Social History of an Indonesian Town* (Cambridge, Mass., 1965); H. Geertz, *The Javanese Family: A Study of Kinship and Socialization* (New York, 1961); R. Jay, *Religion and Politics in Rural Central Java,* Cultural Report Series, #12 (New Haven, 1963); R. Jay, *Javanese Villagers: Social Relations in Rural Modjokuto* (Cambridge, Mass., 1969); E. J. Ryan, "The Value System of a Chinese Community in Java," (Ph.D. diss., Harvard University, 1961). For a later, independent study of the town, see R. I. Wahono, "'Kamar Bola' and 'Waringin': Continuity and Change in a Javanese Town and Its Surroundings" (Ph.D. diss., Australian National University, Canberra, 1984). A recent survey of the region of which Pare is a part is H. Dick, J. J. Fox, and J. Mackie, eds., *Balanced Development: East Java and the New Order* (Oxford, 1993).

5. "The elections were held in 1955": On the elections as such, see H. Feith, *The Indonesian Elections of 1955* (Ithaca, 1957). On the constitu-

tional party regime in general, see H. Feith, *The Decline of Constitutional Democracy in Indonesia* (Ithaca, 1962).

6. *Divina Commedia*: Quoted in J. D. Legge, *Sukarno: A Political Biography* (New York, 1972), p. 4.

7. "When the massacres finally arrived": The best general survey of the massacres is still probably J. Hughes, *Indonesian Upheaval* (New York, 1967). There has been of course much dispute about the causes and scale of the killings. Robert Cribb, ed., *The Indonesian Killings, 1965–66* (Clayton, Australia, 1990), p. 12, summarizes 39 published estimates, ranging from 78,000 to two million dead. On East Java, where Pare is located, see pp. 63–99, esp. p. 83, and 169–176, esp. p. 173. See also Wahono, *Continuity and Change,* for some qualitative material on Pare. For my own contemporary reactions to the events, see C. Geertz, "Are the Javanese Mad?" *Encounter* 26 (1966): 86–88, a response to a piece by H. Leuthy, "Indonesia Confronted," *Encounter* 25 (1965): 80–89, and 26 (1966): 75–83, rather suggesting that they were; Leuthy's reply to me is at 26 (1966): 88–90.

12. "Earlier experience-seekers": Johannes Leo Africanus, *Description de l'Afrique,* 2 vols. (Paris, 1956); Vicomte de Foucauld, *La reconnaissance au Maroc,* 2 vols. (Paris, 1888), vol. 1, p. 37; Edith Wharton, *In Morocco* (New York, 1984), p. 96. For the writings of myself and my colleagues on Sefrou, see, inter alia, T. Dichter, "The Problem of How to Act on an Undefined Stage: An Exploration of Culture, Change, and Individual Consciousness in the Moroccan Town of Sefrou, with a Focus on Three Modern Schools" (Ph.D. diss., University of Chicago, 1976); C. Geertz, H. Geertz, and L. Rosen, *Meaning and Order in Moroccan Society: Three Essays in Cultural Analysis* (Cambridge, 1979); P. Rabinow, *Symbolic Domination: Cultural Form and Historical Change in Morocco* (Chicago, 1975); P. Rabinow, *Reflections on Fieldwork* (Berkeley, 1977); L. Rosen, "The Structure of Social Groups in a Moroccan City" (Ph.D. diss., University of Chicago, 1968); L. Rosen, *Bargaining for Reality: The Construction of Social Relations in a Muslim Community* (Chicago, 1984); L. Rosen, *The Anthropology of Justice* (Cambridge, 1989).

16. "The eloquent statistic": For most of these figures, see H. Benhalima, "Sefrou: De la tradition des Dir à l'intégration économique moderne: Étude de géographie urbaine" (thesis, Montpellier, 1977). I am indebted to Muhammed Benyakhlef for the 1970 census figures. The town today may be getting on toward 70,000 and has been raised to the level of a provincial capital (L. Rosen, personal communication).

20. "Tom Swift": R. Wilbur, "Folk Tune," in *The Beautiful Changes and Other Poems* (New York, 1947), p. 27.

2. Countries

23. "Similarity and difference": World Bank, *World Development Report 1991* (New York, 1991); World Bank, *Trends in Developing Economies* (Washington, D.C., 1991); World Bank, *The World Bank Atlas, 1991* (Washington, D.C., 1991). The "three hundred and fifty years" of Dutch control over Indonesia is a bit of a myth: firm control outside Java was mainly secured in the last century and in some places only in the beginning of this one. Similarly for Morocco: parts of the Atlases were not "pacified" until the 1920s.

25–26. "Books on these countries": H. W. Jones, *Indonesia: The Possible Dream* (New York, 1971); R. Leveau, *Le fellah marocain: Défenseur du trône* (Paris, 1976); K'tut Tantri, *Revolt in Paradise* (London, 1960); J. Waterbury, *The Commander of the Faithful* (London, 1970). For an extremely strong version of the sultanic perspective for Morocco, see M. E. Coombs-Schilling, *Sacred Performances: Islam, Sexuality, and Sacrifice* (New York, 1989); for a study which places the king's authority in a broader, sociologically more realistic context, see A. Hammoudi, *Maître et disciple: Aux fondements culturels de l'autoritarisme marocain* (Paris, 1992). For a strong version of (failed) Indonesian revolutionism, see B. Anderson, *Language and Power: Exploring Political Cultures in Indonesia* (Ithaca, 1990); for a more balanced view, D. K. Emmerson, *Indonesia's Elite: Political Culture and Cultural Politics* (Ithaca, 1976). For my own views, C. Geertz, *Islam Observed* (Chicago, 1973).

27. "divided into islands": For a general survey of Indonesian "ethnic" divisions, see H. Geertz, "Indonesian Cultures and Communities," in R. McVey, *Indonesia* (New Haven, 1963), pp. 24–96. See also J. L. Peacock, *Indonesia: An Anthropological Perspective* (Pacific Palisades, Calif., 1972); C. Geertz, "The Integrative Revolution: Primordial Sentiments and Civil Politics in the New States," in C. Geertz, ed., *Old Societies and New States* (New York, 1964), pp. 105–157; C. Geertz, "'Ethnic Conflict': Three Alternative Terms," *Common Knowledge* 2, no. 3 (1993): 54–65.

31. "Californian seclusion": See W. D. Swearingen, *Moroccan Mirages: Agrarian Dreams and Deceptions, 1912–1986* (Princeton, 1987), p. 59.

31. "the royalist who gave an empire": The phrase is from Princess Marthe Bibesco, quoted in A. Maurois, *Lyautey* (New York, 1931), epigraph and p. 258.

33. "inflated corps": D. Porch, *The Conquest of Morocco* (New York, 1983), p. 298.

33. "one of those officials": J. Berque, *Le Maghreb entre deux guerres* (Paris, 1962), pp. 225ff.

34. "the efforts of Hassan II": I. W. Zartman, "King Hassan's New Mo-

rocco," pp. 1–33, in I. W. Zartman, ed., *The Political Economy of Morocco* (New York, 1987).

34. "Henceforth": Quoted in H. D. Nelson, ed., *Morocco: A Country Study,* 4th ed. (Washington, D.C.: U.S. Govt. Printing Office, 1978), p. 79.

34. "having invented the carrack": J. Law, "On the Methods of Long-distance Control: Vessels, Navigation and the Portuguese Route to India," in J. Law, ed., *Power, Action and Belief: A New Sociology of Knowledge?* (London, 1986), pp. 234–263.

34. "islands full of kings and spices": The term "Moluccas," or more exactly "Maluku," comes from the Arabic, *Jazīrat al-Mulūk,* "islands of kings." I have used Western terms for such places as Borneo, the Celebes, and the Moluccas, rather than the Indonesian ones, only for clarity. On this whole development, see A. Reid, *Southeast Asia in the Age of Commerce, 1450–1680,* vol. 1 (New Haven, 1988).

35. "a Dutch historian": J. C. van Leur, *Indonesian Trade and Society, Essays in Asian Social and Economic History* (The Hague, 1955). For the "greatest trading company," K. Glamann, *Dutch Asiatic Trade, 1620–1740* (The Hague, 1958), p. 1. For other materials on early Southeast Asian trade see M. A. P. Meilink-Roelofsz, *Asian Trade and European Influence in the Indonesian Archipelago between 1500 and about 1630* (The Hague, 1962); B. Schrieke, *Indonesian Sociological Studies,* part I (The Hague, 1955); A. Reid, *Southeast Asia in the Age of Commerce.*

36. "exports": Export percentage of GNP calculated from World Bank, *World Development Report, 1988,* tables 1 and 11, and World Bank, *Trends in Developing Economies 1992* (Washington, D.C., 1992).

37. "*Indisch* life": E. Breton de Nijs, *Tempoe Doeloe* (Amsterdam, 1973); W. F. Wertheim, *Indonesian Society in Transition* (The Hague, 1959), pp. 173ff.

37. "Two hundred sugar factories": Sugar figures are from G. C. Allen and A. G. Donnithorne, *Western Enterprise in Indonesia and Malaya* (New York, 1957), pp. 84ff. For coffee, pp. 89ff; tea (mostly West Javanese), pp. 100ff.

38. "an intra-Javanese phenomenon": There were, of course, also massacres in Bali and in certain parts of North Sumatra. Sukarno died, bereft of power, in 1970. Suharto took official power in March 1966.

40. "New Order Indonesia has been called": On (some of) the varieties of classification of New Order Indonesia, see R. Robison, *Indonesia: The Rise of Capital* (Winchester, Mass., 1986), pp. 105–130.

3. Cultures

42. "the concept of culture": For the global, evolutionary view, see G. Stocking, *Victorian Anthropology* (New York, 1987); for the life-way para-

digm, C. Kluckhohn, *Mirror for Man: The Relation of Anthropology to Modern Life* (New York, 1949).

43. "the Indonesian scholar": T. Abdullah, "Islam and the Formation of Tradition in Indonesia: A Comparative Perspective," *Itinerario* 13, no. 1 (1989): 18.

43–44. "people studies": C. Kluckhohn and D. Leighton, *The Navaho* (New York, 1962), rev. ed. by L. H. Wales and R. Kluckhohn; E. E. Evans-Pritchard, *The Nuer* (Oxford, 1940); B. Malinowski, *The Argonauts of the Western Pacific* (New York, 1920); R. F. Barton, *Ifugao Law* (1919; Berkeley, 1969); W. Rivers, *The Todas* (1906; Oosterhout, 1967); R. Firth, *We, The Tikopia* (London, 1936).

44. "community studies": R. Redfield, *Tepotzlan, a Mexican Village: A Study of Folk Life* (Chicago, 1930); J. Embree, *Suya Mura, a Japanese Village* (Chicago, 1964); J. Pitt-Rivers, *The People of the Sierra* (London, 1954).

46. "was trying to say": B. L. Whorf, *Language, Thought, and Reality, Selected Writings,* ed. J. B. Carroll (Cambridge, Mass., 1956); L. Wittgenstein, *Philosophical Investigations* (New York, 1953): "Every sign *by itself* seems dead. *What* gives it life?—In use it is *alive.* Is life breathed into it there?—Or is the *use* its life?" para. 452, p. 128e.

46. "The languages as such": Javanese is quite simple morphologically, with only a few affixes, applied in more or less regular fashion to unchanging roots, and there are not only no inflections for gender, but none for tense, number, or case either. It is, however, replete with word forms that have, in addition to their primary meaning—"house," "desire," "rice," "you"—a status meaning laid on top of them, such that one can barely utter a sentence in which the relationship between oneself and one's interlocutor (or oneself and someone one is referring to) is not expressed, in a highly calibrated form, throughout the whole. Moroccan Arabic is morphologically extraordinarily complex, as well as irregular. It has inflections, usually multiple, for everything from tense and number to attributive adjectives and verbal nouns. Verbs, nouns, pronouns, and adjectives alike are marked for binary, his and hers, gender, so that, again, barely a sentence can be uttered without invoking it. Status forms, so far as I can see, are wholly absent, even among pronouns, though some people raise their speech register a bit in upscale situations by dropping in classicized words. The king, himself, is just plain "he" *(huwa),* something as against the grain for a Javanese as referring to him, Javanese style, with (an elevated) sex-neutral pronoun *(piyambakipun),* would be for a Moroccan. On Javanese, see W. Keeler, *Javanese: A Cultural Approach* (Athens, Ohio, 1984); on Moroccan Arabic, R. S. Harrell, *A Short Reference Grammar of Moroccan Arabic* (Washington, D.C., 1962).

47. "Javanese are preoccupied": L. H. Palmier, *Social Status and Power in Java* (London, 1960); C. Geertz, *The Religion of Java* (Glencoe, Ill., 1960),

part 3; J. Siegel, *Solo in the New Order; Language and Hierarchy in an Indonesian City* (Princeton, 1986).

47. "an ontological wall": H. Geertz, "The Meaning of Family Ties," in C. Geertz et al., *Meaning and Order in Moroccan Society* (Cambridge, 1978), pp. 315–379; L. Rosen, "The Negotiation of Reality: Male-Female Relations in Sefrou, Morocco," in L. Beck and N. Keddie, eds., *Women in the Muslim World* (Cambridge, Mass., 1979), pp. 561–584; M. E. Coombs-Schilling, *Sacred Performances: Islam, Sexuality, and Sacrifice* (New York, 1989); F. Mernissi, *Beyond the Veil* (New York, 1975); A. Hammoudi, *La victime et ses masques: Essai sur le sacrifice et la mascarade au Maghreb* (Paris, 1988); A. Hammoudi, *Maître et disciple: Aux fondements culturels de l'autoritarisme marocain* (Paris, forthcoming).

53–54. "Islam came to the archipelago": There is still no integral study of the Islamization of Indonesia. For summaries and speculations, M. Ricklefs, "Six Centuries of Islamization in Java," in N. Levtzion, ed., *Conversion to Islam* (London, 1979), pp. 100–128; G. Drewes, "New Light on the Coming of Islam to Indonesia," *Bijdragen tot de Taal-, Land-, en Volkenkunde* 124 (1968): 433–459; A. Johns, "Sufism as a Category in Indonesian Literature and History," *Journal of Southeast Asian History* 2 (1961): 10–23. On the "Hindu" period, G. Coedès, *The Indianized States of Southeast Asia* (Honolulu, 1958). Materials on the pre-Hindu period remain scarce and specialized. For summaries, see K.-C. Chang, "Major Problems in the Culture History of Southeast Asia," *Bulletin of the Institute of Ethnology: Academica Sinica* 13 (1992): 1–23; W. Solheim II, "The 'New Look' of Southeast Asian Prehistory," *Journal of the Siam Society* 60 (1972): 1–20.

55. "The book I wrote": C. Geertz, *The Religion of Java* (Glencoe, Ill., 1960).

56. "What has come to be known": R. Liddle, *Politics and Culture in Indonesia* (Ann Arbor, 1988), pp. 12ff. For a book that swallows this view of things whole, and to which the references to Meccan kratons and Sufi theocracies refer, see M. Woodward, *Islam in Java: Normative Piety and Mysticism in the Sultanate of Yogyakarta* (Tucson, 1989).

56–57. "ahli kebatinan": See Geertz, *Religion of Java*, part 3; Liddle, *Politics and Culture in Indonesia*, pp. 14ff.

57. "a patch sample for a general weave": For a more extensive comparison of Islam in Indonesia and Morocco, see C. Geertz, *Islam Observed: Religious Development in Morocco and Indonesia* (New Haven, 1968).

57. "the bearers of Islam": The so-called Arab invasions of Morocco remain speculative and ill-documented. For brief summaries, see *Morocco: A Country Study* (Washington, D.C., 1978) 4th ed., pp. 17ff.; N. Barbour, *Morocco* (London, 1965). For Rome, etc., see these and J. Abun-Nasr, *A History of the Maghrib* (Cambridge, 1971), pp. 13ff.

58. "Nor—Jews, never much more than": S. Deshen, *The Mellah Society, Jewish Community Life in Sherifian Morocco* (Chicago, 1989).

58. "no Epsom, nor Ascot": H. James, *Hawthorne* (New York, 1870), pp. 42–43.

59. "cultural fault lines": See, inter alia, A. Bel, *La religion musulmane en Berbèrie* (Paris, 1938); Geertz, *Islam Observed;* R. Montagne, *Les Berbères et le Makhzen dans le sud du Maroc* (Paris, 1930); A. Hammoudi, "Segmentarité, stratification sociales, pouvoir et sainteté," *Hesperis-Tamuda* 16 (1974): 147–180; A. Hammoudi, "Sainteté, pouvoir, et société," *Annales: Économies, sociétés, civilisations* 35 (1980): 615–649; J. Berque, *Ulémas, fondateurs, insurgés du Maghreb* (Paris, 1978). D. Eickelman, *Knowledge and Power in Morocco: The Education of a Twentieth Century Notable* (Princeton, 1985); D. Eickelman, *Moroccan Islam: Tradition and Society in a Pilgrimage Center* (Austin, 1976). For Ibn Khaldun, *The Muqaddimah,* trans. F. Rosenthal, 3 vols. (London, 1958). For some recent discussions of the functioning of "religious personages" within the general political structure of Morocco, see Hammoudi, *Maître et disciple;* H. Elboudrari, *La "Maison du Cautionnement": Les shurfa d'Ouezzane de la sainteté à la puissance, étude d'anthropologie religieuse et politique (Maroc, XVIIᵉ—XXᵉ s.)* (Ph.D. diss., Ecole des Hautes Etudes en Sciences Sociales, Paris, 1984).

60. "so it looks to us now": For some recent views of sixteenth-century developments, see M. Garcia-Arenal, "*Mahdî, Murâbit, Sharîf:* L'avènement de la dynastie Sa'dienne," *Studia Islamica* 71 (1990): 77–114; M. Garcia-Arenal, "Sainteté et pouvoir dynastique au Maroc: La résistance de Fès aux Sa'diens," *Annales: Économies, sociétés, civilisations* 4 (1990): 1019–1042; A. Bouchareb, "Les conséquences socio-culturelles de la conquête ibérique du littoral marocain," *Actas del Coloquio de la Peninsula Iberica con el Magreb* (Madrid, 1988).

61. "the verb is causative": On the "-i" verbal suffix in Javanese, see Keeler, *Javanese: A Cultural Approach,* pp. 126ff. On Moroccan imperatives, Harrell, *A Short Reference Grammar of Moroccan Arabic,* pp. 175–176.

62. "the fact that facts are made": See B. Latour, *Science in Action: How to Follow Scientists and Engineers through Society* (Cambridge, Mass., 1987).

4. Hegemonies

64. "The ends of the earth": On the general problem of the representation of the anthropologist in ethnographic texts, see C. Geertz, *Works and Lives: The Anthropologist as Author* (Stanford, 1988).

66. "It is dawn": On the town in which we were living, see C. Geertz, *Peddlers and Princes* (Chicago, 1963); C. Geertz, *Negara: The Theatre State in Nineteenth Century Bali* (Princeton, 1980); C. Geertz, *Bali: Interprétation*

d'une culture (Paris, 1983); J. Boon, *The Anthropological Romance of Bali, 1597–1972* (Cambridge, 1977).

67–68. "a famous sixteenth-century battle": On this, L. Valensi, *Fables de la mémoire: La glorieuse bataille des trois rois* (Paris, 1992).

68. "Emily was an Englishwoman": Emily, Shareefa of Wazan, *My Life Story* (London, 1912).

68. On Wezzan (often spelled Ouezzane, Ouazzan, or even Wazan) and the Wazzaniyya (Tayyibiyya), see E. Aubin, *Morocco of To-Day* (London, 1906), pp. 36—392. For a vivid eyewitness description of the character of the place and the sheikhly family in Emily's times, see W. B. Harris, *The Morocco that Was* (Edinburgh and London, 1921), pp. 273–284. For a religio-political history of the brotherhood as such, see H. Elboudrari, "La 'Maison du Cautionnement': Les shurfa d'Ouezzane de la sainteté à la puissance, étude d'anthropologie religieuse et politique (Maroc, XVIIᵉ-XXᵉ s.)" (Ph.D. diss., Ecole des Hautes Etudes en Sciences Sociales, Paris, 1984). On the founding "saint" of the brotherhood, see also H. Elboudrari, "Quand les saints font les villes: Lecture anthropologique de la pratique d'un saint marocain du XVIIème siècle," *Annales: Économies, sociétés, civilizations* 3 (1985): 489–508; H. Elboudrari, "Allégeance, ordre et constance: L'éthique d'un saint fondateur maghrébin," in H. Elboudrari, ed., *Modes de transmission et la culture religieuse en Islam* (Cairo, 1992), pp. 261–280. I had myself thought at one point of working there. After being stoned in the medina, albeit inaccurately, I thought perhaps not. A colleague, John Napora, worked there in the 1980s, but on the weavers' community: none of the sharifs save, at arm's length, the sheikh, would talk to him.

69. "the invading Americans": On the "American period" in Kenitra, see L. B. Blair, *Western Window in the Arab World* (Austin, 1970). As Blair, then a naval lieutenant commander, was the U.S. politico-military liaison officer in Morocco and does not mention Hassan, his representation of his role there (as well of his role in the Independence crisis, the numerous historians of which also do not mention him) should perhaps be taken with a grain of salt.

70. "how much we say": Hugo von Hofmannsthal, "Twilight of the Outward Life," trans. P. Viereck, in S. Rodman, ed., *One Hundred Modern Poems* (New York, 1951), pp. 31–32.

71. "a regionalist rebellion": An integral history of the rebellion—PRRI-Permesta—which was centered both in West Sumatra and the Northern Celebes, does not, so far as I know, exist. For an account of the Celebes part of the affair, see B. S. Harvey, *Permesta: Half a Rebellion* (Ithaca, 1977). For the view from the American embassy see the memoirs of the then-ambassador there (though he arrived a bit after the rebellion began), H. P. Jones, *Indonesia: The Possible Dream* (New York, 1971), esp. pp. 67–85, 113–146. See also D. Lev, *The Transition to Guided Democracy: Indonesian Politics, 1957–*

59 (Ithaca, 1966). For an at-the-time journalistic report, see W. A. Hanna, *Bung Karno's Indonesia, Part VII: The Rebel Cause, October 9, 1959* (New York, 1961).

74. "the first civilian plane": The reason we were able to leave so soon, and indeed were more or less obliged to, is that the Javanese head of the invading army happened to be someone I had known earlier in Jogjakarta, and realizing that my wife and I could speak Javanese and were quartered among his troops, he wanted us out of there.

75. "I was invited": A second conference, matching this one on a home-and-home basis, was held at the Wye Plantation in Queenstown, Maryland, in May of the same year, to which came, in addition to most of the Marrakech participants, the president of Long Island University, the chairman of Sears World Trade, and the Moroccan ambassador to the United States. My recollections of the conference have been much assisted by an unpublished summary of its proceedings prepared by its rapporteur, Dr. Bruce Lawrence of Duke University, though he is of course not responsible for either their tone or their content. Aside from myself there were about a half-dozen other academics, both Moroccan and American, in attendance.

79. "a place called Aceh": For a brief summary of Achenese regional politics to 1953, see E. Morris, "Social Revolution and the Islamic Vision," in A. Kahin, ed., *Regional Dynamics of the Indonesian Revolution: Unity from Diversity* (Honolulu, 1985), pp. 82–110. On the colonial war, P. van't Veer, *De Atjeh-oorlog* (Amsterdam, 1969); C. Snouck-Hurgronje, *The Achenese*, 2 vols. (Leiden, 1906); and J. Siegel, *The Rope of God* (Berkeley and Los Angeles, 1969), which also has a discussion of developments in the 1950s and 1960s (concerning the latter, see also B. Dahm, *History of Indonesia in the Twentieth Century* (London, 1971), pp. 167–168). For events during the Revolution, see A. Reid, *The Blood of the People* (Oxford, 1979), esp. chs. 2, 4, 7. The nineties upheaval seems to be an unclear mixture of drug smuggling, anti-Javanese sentiment, and resistance to central military control: see Indonesian News Service, Lanham-Seabrook, Md., reports nos. 270, 271, 272, November 27, 29, December 1, 1992.

79. "I was a technical consultant": The plan, which I put together after returning to the United States, was for four or five such research stations at promising locations outside of Jakarta, and for the most part outside of Java, each of which was to be headed for a year at a time by an established Western (i.e., American, European, or Australian) scholar and a senior Indonesian scholar working in harness, to which a half-dozen or so junior Indonesian scholars from other regions of the archipelago would be seconded, also for a year, to carry out supervised empirical research in the locality involved. The stations, which eventually amounted to, I think, four, were indeed set up, under the supervision of an Indonesian committee, and for twenty years were

a significant force in the formation of what is, by now, an impressive social science community in Indonesia. Beginning in the late 1980s, they began to be disbanded, local university institutions having grown to be able to take over their functions. For my original report, see C. Geertz, "Social Science Policy in a New State: A Programme for the Stimulation of the Social Sciences in Indonesia," *Minerva* 12 (1974): 365–381.

81. "My known interest": C. Geertz, *The Religion of Java* (Glencoe, Ill., 1960), part 2; C. Geertz, "Modernization in a Muslim Society: The Indonesian Case," in R. N. Bellah, ed., *Religion and Progress in Modern Asia* (New York, 1966), pp. 93–108.

82. "the higher levels of religious scholarship": *Fiqh* is Islamic "jurisprudence"; *tafsīr* is "commentary," especially upon the Quran; *usūl* is, more or less, "basic principles," most especially *tauḥid,* the oneness of Allah; *taṣawwuf* is "mystical learning and practice."

83. "Nimrod was an atheist": Nimrod is not in fact mentioned by name in the Quran, though there are various allusions to him in connection with his disputes with Ibrahim, and a number of commentators, notably Tabari, mention him. There are, as well, a number of legends about him in Muslim literature, including the arrow-shooting one, which ends with him growing suddenly aged after his boast to have killed God and being forthwith killed by a gnat. See "Namrūd," in H. A. R. Gibb and J. H. Kramers, *Shorter Encyclopaedia of Islam* (Leiden and London, 1961), pp. 437–438.

84. "the oldest city in Morocco": Edith Wharton, *In Morocco* (1920; London and New York, 1984), pp. 75–76, 77. Not everyone thinks so: Sefrouis are fond of quoting (apocryphally) the supposed founder of Fez, Idris I: "I am leaving the city of Sefrou for the village of Fez."

85. "its unmatchable civilization": For the romantic view of Fez, see T. Burckhardt, *Fez: City of Islam* (Cambridge, 1992). For recent, UNESCO-sponsored efforts to restore the city ("We must rebuild Fez. It is a universal city"), see J. Martin, "Fez, Preserving a City," *Aramco World,* May–June 1993, pp. 20–27.

86. "a descendant of the Prophet immigrant from Arabia": On the foundation of Fez and the presumed role of Moulay Idris I in it, see J. Brignon et al., *Histoire du Maroc* (Paris, 1967), pp. 63–64.

87. "the Eton of the Moroccan political elite": J. Waterbury, *The Commander of the Faithful* (London, 1970), p. 101, where a list of prominent nationalist leaders graduated from the college is given. Moulay Idris (founded in 1912) was only one, though probably the most important, of the Collèges Franco-Musulmans the Lyautey regime set up: others being at Casablanca (1914), Marrakech (1914), Rabat (1921), and Meknes (1929), of which perhaps only the one in Rabat, Moulay Youssef, rivaled Moulay Idris in significance (in 1917 there were 150 students in Fez, 96 in Rabat, and though

enrollments doubtless increased as the Protectorate wore on, this was always a very small elite); J. Halstead, *Rebirth of a Nation, The Origins and Rise of Moroccan Nationalism* (Cambridge, Mass., 1967), pp. 105–109. For statistical information on the role of Moulay Idris and the other collèges, as well as their alumni associations, in the formation of the national political elite, see R. Leveau, *Le fellah Marocain: Défenseur du trône* (Paris, 1976), pp. 171, 183, 184, 221–222, 186–190.

89. "In 1950 there were fifty-eight": Calculated, as is the 1980 figure, from *The Concise Columbia Encyclopedia,* 2nd ed. (New York, 1989), p. 852. Today (1993), there are 182 (183 as soon as Eritrea gets in), ranging from St. Kitts and Nevis at 260 square kilometers to the Russian Federation at 17 million (or if you prefer your comparisons demographic, from St. Kitts at 47,000 inhabitants to China at a billion plus).

90. "a mere tabulation": Morocco: On the border wars with Algeria, see *Morocco: A Country Study* (Washington, D.C., 1978), p. 256; for a Moroccan view, A. Ouardighi, *Le Maroc de la mort de Mohammed V à la Guerre des Sables* (Rabat, n.d.). On the American bases, see I. W. Zartman, *Morocco: Problems of a New Power* (New York, 1964), pp. 23–60; Blair, *Western Window in the Arab World.* On the Ben Barka affair, see G. Perrault, *Notre ami le Roi* (Paris, 1990), pp. 93–108. On the two coups, ibid., pp. 117–140, 151–173. On the Saharan war, Polisario, etc., see J. Damis, *Conflict in Northwest Africa: The Western Sahara Dispute* (Stanford, 1983); T. Hodges, *Western Sahara: The Roots of a Desert War* (Westport, Conn., 1983). Indonesia: On the Bandung Conference, see G. McT. Kahin, *The Asian-African Conference, Bandung, Indonesia, April 1955* (Ithaca, 1956); J. D. Legge, *Sukarno, A Political Biography* (New York, 1972), pp. 262–266. On the regional rebellion, see Harvey, *Permesta.* On the West New Guinea crisis, see J. A. C. Mackie, *Konfrontasi: The Indonesia-Malaysia Dispute, 1963–66* (London, 1974), pp. 98–103. On "Confrontation with Malaysia," ibid., passim. On the coup see the appropriate notes in Chapter 1 above. For a general account of Indonesian foreign policy during the Sukarno years by a former foreign minister, see Ide Anak Gde Agung, *Twenty Years Indonesian Foreign Policy, 1945–65* (The Hague, 1973). An unpolemical book on the Timor affair is difficult to find, but J. Dunn, *Timor: A People Betrayed* (Auckland, 1983) gives a general outline of the course of events.

On Japan, see Y. Tsurumi, "Japanese Investments in Indonesia: Ownership, Technology Transfer and Political Conflict," in G. F. Papanek, ed., *The Indonesian Economy* (New York, 1980), pp. 295–323. On labor migration, T. Gerholm and Y. G. Lithman, eds., *The New Islamic Presence in Western Europe* (London, 1988); L. Tahla et al., *Maghrébins en France: Émigrés ou immigrés?* (Paris, 1983); on oil, see I. Palmer, *The Indonesian Economy Since 1965* (London, 1978), pp. 137–151. On the green revolution, see L. A. Mears and S. Moeljono, "Food Policy," in A. Booth and P. McCawley, *The Indonesian Economy during the Soeharto Era* (London, 1981), pp. 23–61; S. Pearson et al., *Rice Policy in Indonesia* (Ithaca, 1991). For an evocation of the atmospherics of the Cold War throughout this period, see F. Inglis, *The Cruel Peace* (New York, 1991).

5. Disciplines

96. "My dictionary": *The American Heritage Dictionary of the English Language* (New York, 1969), p. 378. *The Compact Edition of the Oxford English Dictionary,* vol. I (Oxford, 1971), pp. 415–417. On the play of the penal and pedagogical meaning of "discipline," which pervades much of the work of Michel Foucault, see especially his *Discipline and Punish* (New York, 1978).

99. "pursuits in a calling": For an informal discussion of some of the matters discussed in the remainder of this chapter, see Richard Handler, "An Interview with Clifford Geertz," *Current Anthropology* 32 (1991): 603–613.

99. "presidential address": T. Parsons, "The Prospects of Sociological Theory," in his *Essays in Sociological Theory,* rev. ed. (Glencoe, Ill., 1954), pp. 348–369; quotation at p. 349.

100. "The Social Relations Department": The major animators were the sociologist (and first chairman of the department) Talcott Parsons (b. 1902), the social psychologist Gordon Allport (b. 1897), the clinical psychologist Henry A. Murray (b. 1893), the anthropologist Clyde Kluckhohn (b. 1905), and the sociologist Samuel Stouffer (b. 1900). I was admitted to the department (as was my then wife, Hildred Geertz) in 1950 and received my doctorate (as did she) in 1956. I also taught there for a year (1956–57) after returning from the field.

100. "call to arms": T. Parsons et al., "Toward a Common Language for the Areas of the Social Sciences," unpublished memorandum. The general program of the department was later laid out in a more extensive fashion in T. Parsons and E. Shils, eds., *Toward a General Theory of Action* (Cambridge, Mass., 1951). The established Psychology and Anthropology Departments remained in being; Sociology was wholly absorbed into the new department.

100. "The Russian Research Center": The center was not properly part of the department, but it was dominated by and fairly well identified with it at that point in time.

101. "The day I arrived": Here and throughout this chapter, the use of "I" should much of the time be "we," for the involvement of my then wife, Hildred Geertz, in it all was largely identical to my own. However, because I do not want to ascribe my views, perceptions, attitudes, or whatever to her, to write in her name, I have stuck to the first-person singular for the most

part, only resorting to the "we" in places where it is unavoidable and there is no question of the appropriation of someone else's voice involved. This is a difficult "text construction" issue, which I am not sure I have satisfactorily solved. Suffice it to say that I was never alone, emotionally or intellectually, in any of this, and my debts to Hildred Geertz are no less massive for being inexplicit.

102. "the five cultures project": On the five cultures (Navajo, Zuni, Spanish American, Mormon, and "Texan") project, first called the Ramah Project, later the Rimrock Project, see E. M. Albert and E. Z. Vogt, eds., *The People of Rimrock* (Cambridge, Mass., 1966). My own contribution was an unpublished study, "Death, Drought, and Alcoholism in Five Southwestern Cultures," on file in the Peabody Museum Library at Harvard University.

103. "team field project": The members of the team were Alice Dewey (anthropologist), Donald Fagg (sociologist), Clifford Geertz (anthropologist), Hildred Geertz (anthropologist), Robert Jay (anthropologist), John Rodriguez (social psychologist), Edward Ryan (anthropologist), Thomas Plaut (clinical psychologist), and Lea Williams (historian). Only Dewey, Fagg, Clifford and Hildred Geertz, Jay, and Ryan in the event worked in the field site. Douglas Oliver, the professor in the Anthropology Department who did the original organizing and planning of the project, dropped out before we left for the field; he was replaced by Rufus Hendon, a linguist from Yale. The funding of the project was provided by the Ford Foundation.

103. "the revolutionary university": Gadjah (or as it would now be spelled, Gajah) Mada, named after the famous prime minister of Majapahit, had its origins during the Revolution when Jogjakarta was the Republican capital. It has since much expanded and moved to a new campus, but at that time it was still housed in the sultan's palace, and was small, vaguely organized, and uncertain of its direction.

104–105. "the immediate problem": It is to be understood that I give here, and throughout, my view of what happened colored by my feelings at the time, now recollected more or less in tranquility, but unaltered. Others in the group would perhaps give different accounts.

105. "the professors": The professors from the Indonesian side were Djojodigoeno, a customary law scholar, Iso Reksohadipradja, an agricultural economist, and Prihoetomo, a linguist. Despite the tensions described in text, I had very warm and supportive relations with Professor Djojodigoeno in later years, and Professor Iso Reksohadipradja was all the way through, even in the difficult times, personally understanding and helpful. Professor Prihoetomo was ill and played little role.

106–107. "the moral crux": For discussions, see J. Clifford, *The Predicament of Culture: Twentieth-Century Ethnography, Literature, and Art* (Cambridge, Mass., 1989); J. Clifford and G. Marcus, eds., *Writing Culture: The*

Poetics and Politics of Ethnography (Berkeley, 1986); G. Marcus and M. Fischer, *Anthropology as Cultural Critique: An Experimental Moment in the Human Sciences* (Chicago, 1986); C. Geertz, *Works and Lives: The Anthropologist as Author* (Stanford, 1988).

110. "the settling in of a general direction": For a frankly whiggish, history of ideas account of developments in anthropological thought over the last thirty years, in some ways parallel, in more orthogonal, to the episodical and experiential "disciplinary communities" approach taken here, see S. Ortner, "Theory in Anthropology since the Sixties," *Comparative Studies in Society and History* 26 (1984): 126–166.

112. "a foundational essay": E. Shils, "On the Comparative Study of the New States," in C. Geertz, ed., *Old Societies and New States, The Quest for Modernity in Asia and Africa* (New York, 1963), p. 8.

113. "some thirteen members": The core members of the committee were E. Shils (sociology, India); D. Apter (political science, Ghana and Uganda); L. A. Fallers (anthropology, Uganda and Turkey); M. Marriott (anthropology, India); M. Janowitz (sociology; comparative study of the military); L. Binder (political science, Pakistan, Iran, and Egypt); M. Nash (anthropology, Guatemala, Burma, and Malaysia); H. Johnson (economics, foreign trade and development); C. A. Anderson (education, comparative education); M. Rheinstein (law, comparative law); R. LeVine (anthropology, Nigeria, Kenya); A. Zolberg (political science, the Ivory Coast), and me. All these people continued as full-time members of their several departments, except for me. Though I was officially a member of the Anthropology Department, I was, for the first five years, free to devote all my energies to the committee, of which I became, after a while, first executive secretary and then chairman. For a general description of the workings of the committee, see Apter's preface to *Old Societies and New States*.

114. "a consideration of more general intellectual trends": Virtually all the members of the Department of Anthropology were actively involved in these discussions, which continued on a regular and formal basis for several years. My own interactions were perhaps most intense and continuous with Lloyd Fallers and David Schneider, both of whom had come, more or less coincidentally, to Chicago from Berkeley at the same time that I did; with Milton Singer, a philosopher and disciple of Robert Redfield turned South Asian anthropologist; and later on with Victor Turner, moved to Chicago from Cornell. The whole enterprise was presided over by a most benevolent senior faculty, most notably Fred Eggan, Sol Tax, Robert Braidwood, and Norman McQuown, all of whom may have at times wondered what they had let loose, and included most prominently McKim Marriott, Manning Nash, Robert McC. Adams, Clark Howell, and later on Melford Spiro and Nur Yallman. It was, all in all, the most beneficent and supportive, as well as the most

stimulating, academic environment I have ever experienced; for the students too seemed extraordinarily energized. On the "hermeneutic" or "interpretive" movement in the human sciences more generally, see P. Rabinow and W. M. Sullivan, eds., *Interpretive Social Science* (Berkeley, 1979); P. Rabinow and W. M. Sullivan, eds., *Interpretive Social Science: A Second Look* (Berkeley, 1987); for the anthropological dimension of it, J. L. Dolgin, D. S. Kemnitzer, and D. M. Schneider, eds., *Symbolic Anthropology: A Reader in the Study of Symbols and Meanings* (New York, 1977); see also M. Singer, "Semiotic Anthropology: A Memoir," in *Encyclopedia of Language and Linguistics* (Edinburgh, 1994). The most accessible statement of my own views is probably C. Geertz, *The Interpretation of Cultures: Selected Essays* (New York, 1973), especially the first chapter, on "thick description," and the last, on the Balinese cockfight. See also my "Blurred Genres: The Refiguration of Social Thought" in C. Geertz, *Local Knowledge: Further Essays in Interpretive Anthropology* (New York, 1983).

116. "a sort of summit conference": The gathering was called Conference on New Approaches in Social Anthropology, and was organized by Professors Max Gluckman of Manchester University and Fred Eggan of the University of Chicago. The results were published in four volumes, M. Banton, ed., *The Relevance of Models for Social Anthropology, Political Systems and the Distribution of Power, Anthropological Approaches to the Study of Religion,* and *The Social Anthropology of Complex Societies* (New York, 1966).

119. "this plan was put into effect": For a list of the main works emerging from the project, see above, note to page 12. The doctoral researchers were Lawrence Rosen, who was in the field in 1966–1967, and worked most especially on social organization and on the local legal system; Paul Rabinow, who was in the field in 1968–1969, and studied a village a few miles from town in which I had done some work earlier on; and Thomas Dichter, who was in the field in 1969–1971, and worked mainly on the school system. A professional photographer, Paul Hyman, spent some weeks with us in 1969. The timing of all this was not absolutely precise, and there were a few gaps during which none of us were there and a few periods in which my wife and I and the students were there together for a somewhat longer time. Both Rosen and I have returned to the town on several occasions since, in my case in 1972, 1976, and 1986, in his in 1969, 1978, and 1991. Dale Eickelman, also then a graduate student at Chicago, studied another town in central Morocco at least generally similar to Sefrou, Boujad, and had a collegial and intellectual, though not a formal, relation to our project. See D. Eickelman, *Moroccan Islam: Tradition and Society in a Pilgrimage Center* (Austin, 1976); D. Eickelman, *Knowledge and Power in Morocco: The Education of a Twentieth-Century Notable* (Princeton, 1986). My research and my wife's was mainly sponsored by a National Institutes of Mental Health Senior Career

Fellowship; the graduate students also had research support from NIMH and various fellowships; and both Rosen and Rabinow wrote up some of their work at the Institute for Advanced Study, Princeton, after I moved there in 1970.

120. "one of them emerged": P. Rabinow, *Reflections on Fieldwork in Morocco* (Berkeley, 1977). For some comments of my own on this type of work, see ch. 4, "I-Witnessing: Malinowski's Children," in C. Geertz, *Works and Lives: The Anthropologist as Author* (Stanford, 1988).

120. "the philanthropical entrepreneur and all-round fixer of things": A. Flexner, *Universities: American, English, German* (Oxford, 1930), pp. 213–214; as quoted in B. M. Stern, "A History of the Institute for Advanced Study, 1930–1950," 2 vols., unpubl., 1964. Stern's lively account of the personal contestations, financial struggles, and institutional vicissitudes, all of them severe, of the first twenty years of the Institute was commissioned by its third director, J. Robert Oppenheimer. When it appeared, however, Oppenheimer decided not to permit it to be published, ostensibly on the grounds that many of the people discussed in it were still alive, but probably because the Institute faculty and trustees were no more attracted to the proposition of telling the truth in a public place than such groups normally are. It has had a semi-subterranean, not to say clandestine, existence since.

For Flexnerian references to the Collège de France, ibid., p. 93: "[The Institute should pursue a policy] analogous to that of the Collège de France, viz., to take advantage of surprises by creating from time to time a chair for a new subject or an unexpected person. By the same token, since the Institute is not concerned with subjects or degrees . . . chairs that have served their purpose can be discontinued. In these respects the stimulating influence of the Collège de France has proved of incalculable value. It has pioneered in every direction . . ."

For All Souls, ibid., p. 90: "In the course of time, the buildings may be so conceived and executed so as to facilitate [free and unstructured] intercourse . . . I have in mind the evolution that in the process of centuries has taken place at All Souls College, Oxford, where, as in the proposed Institute, there are no undergraduate students, and where advanced students and the older Fellows live under ideal conditions, whether for their individual work or for collaboration and cooperation. No one planned all this. It grew up because scholars were left free to work out their own salvation . . . If the spirit of learning animates the Institute . . . men will talk together and work together, because they live together, have their recreation together, meet on the same human social level, and have a single goal." Though the Institute was originally designed to grant doctoral degrees, this aim was quickly abandoned for an entirely post-doctoral, non-degree-granting program.

For another history of the Institute, almost entirely confined to the sciences side of things and mainly concerned with the content of the work done there, see Ed Regis's engaging *Who Got Einstein's Office? Eccentricity and Genius at the Institute for Advanced Study* (Reading, Mass., 1987); cf. A. Borel, "The School of Mathematics at the Institute for Advanced Study," in *A Century of Mathematics in America* (Providence, 1989), part 3, pp. 119–147.

122. "whatever else he may have been": Stern, "History of the Institute," p. 219. Frankfurter continued: "I do not know by what right you may hope for a combination of greater disinterestness *[sic]* and capacity than, say, the Harvard Law School is able to attract, or, let us say, than is now found in the Supreme Court . . . I can assure you that neither of these institutions could be conducted on the assumption that it is a paradise. In both personal interactions play an important part; in both personal sensitiveness has not been wanting because of personal differentiations."

122. "a letter to the Queen of Belgium": The Einstein letter is quoted in L. Y. Jones, Jr., "Bad Days on Mount Olympus: The Big Shoot-out at the Institute for Advanced Study," *Atlantic Monthly,* April 1974, pp. 27–53 at p. 39.

124. "returned to haunt us": I. L. Horowitz, "Trouble in Paradise: The Institute for Advanced Study," *Change* 5 (1979): 44–49; "Trouble in Paradise," *The Economist,* June 7, 1975, pp. 40, 43; "Ivory Tower Tempest," *Time,* March 19, 1973, p. 48; "Thunderbolts on Olympus," *Newsweek,* March 19, 1973, p. 60; W. K. Stuckley, "The Garden of the Lonely Wise: A Profile of the Institute for Advanced Studies *[sic]*," *Science Digest,* February 1975, pp. 28–37; "In the Groves Where Einstein Toiled: Scholars Battle, and the Dialog Isn't Socratic," *National Observer,* March 17, 1973; J. Conway, "Infighting in the Ivory Tower: The Institute for Advanced Studies *[sic]* is an academic paradise. So why can't its faculty seem to get along?" (this had a drawing of baldheaded men with moustaches and beards hitting one another over the head with books), *Parade/The Philadelphia Inquirer,* May 5, 1974, pp. 20–26; D. Shapley, "Institute for Advanced Study: Einstein Is a Hard Act to Follow," *Science,* 179 (1973): 1209–1211; Jones, "Bad Days on Mount Olympus." Other accounts include W. Chapman, "The Battle of Princeton, 1973," *Washington Post,* March 11, 1973; a peculiarly tendentious series of reports by I. Shenker in the *New York Times* in the Spring of 1973; T. Parsons, "Robert Bellah and the Princeton Institute for Advanced Study," *Commonweal,* April 1973; and Regis, *Who Got Einstein's Office?,* the first chapter of which is entitled "The Platonic Heaven." The last chapter, however, introduces a somewhat different note: "Babes in Toyland." Of these accounts, that by Jones is the fullest and most informative; that by Horowitz the most reflective about the nature of the social sciences and their place at the Institute. Shapley, Parsons, and Regis are also useful.

126. "the School, now that it was officially founded": Hirschman retired in 1985, but remains active. As noted, an attempt on the part of the school to appoint another professor, in a field different from those already represented, in 1990–91, was frustrated by an explosion similar to that of the Bellah case. The fellows, all of whom are post-doctoral, are selected by the permanent faculty on the basis of applications. Most (in the social science school, virtually all) come for a year, though there are some multi-year and some six-month appointments as well. The fellows are variously supported—by Institute funds, by outside grants, or by resources of their own. For a sense of the general approach to things of the other members of the social science faculty, see, inter alia, A. O. Hirschman, *The Passions and the Interests: Political Arguments for Capitalism before Its Triumph* (Princeton, 1977); J. Scott, *Gender and the Politics of History* (New York, 1988); M. Walzer, *Spheres of Justice* (New York, 1983).

128. "the story of all this": For characteristic statements of various of these themes, see J. Clifford, "On Ethnographic Authority," *Representations* 1 (1983): 118–146; J. Clifford, *The Predicament of Culture: Twentieth Century Ethnography, Literature, and Art* (Cambridge, Mass., 1988); J. Clifford and G. Marcus, eds., *Writing Culture: The Poetics and Politics of Ethnography* (Berkeley, 1986); G. Marcus and M. Fischer, *Anthropology as Cultural Critique: An Experimental Moment in the Human Sciences* (Chicago, 1986); D. Hymes, ed., *Reinventing Anthropology* (New York, 1969); Talal Asad, ed., *Anthropology and the Colonial Encounter* (New York, 1973); J. Boon, *Other Tribes, Other Scribes: Symbolic Anthropology in the Comparative Study of Cultures, Histories, Religions, and Texts* (Cambridge, 1982); J. Fabian, *Time and the Other: How Anthropology Makes Its Object* (New York, 1983); R. Rosaldo, *Culture and Truth: The Remaking of Social Analysis* (Boston, 1989); M. Manganaro, ed., *Modernist Anthropology: From Fieldwork to Text* (Princeton, 1990); R. G. Fox, ed., *Recapturing Anthropology: Working in the Present* (Santa Fe, 1991); R. Borofsky, ed., *Assessing Cultural Anthropology* (Honolulu, 1994). My own pass at some of these issues can be found in Geertz, *Works and Lives*; C. Geertz, "The Uses of Diversity," *Tanner Lectures,* vol. 7 (Salt Lake City, 1986), pp. 253–275; C. Geertz, "'Local Knowledge and Its Limits': Some *Obiter Dicta,*" *Yale Journal of Criticism* 5 (1992): 129–135, as well as, of course, to be properly self-reflexive amid all this remaking, reinventing, and recapturing, in the whole course of this present work.

132. "When you are there as a petitioning visitor": For some more detailed reflections on these matters, together with examples, see C. Geertz, "Thinking as a Moral Act: Ethical Dimensions of Anthropological Field Work," *Antioch Review* 27 (1968): 134–159.

132. "sheer numbers": For the figures, Borofsky, *Assessing,* p. 13. As elsewhere in this discussion the tacit conflation of "anthropology" and "cul-

tural (or social) anthropology" distorts the picture a bit. But as cultural anthropology has far and away been the fastest-growing component, sorting it out would only dramatize the contrast.

133. "the poet": T. Roethke, "The Waking," in *Words for the Wind: Collected Verse of Theodore Roethke* (New York, 1958), p. 124. What he was talking about, of course, was love.

6. Modernities

136. "The commanding categories": On the appearance of the word "modern" in English, see the word history note under that entry in *The American Heritage Dictionary of the English Language,* 3rd ed. (Boston, 1992), p. 1161. Modern reflections on the modern are, of course, extremely numerous: for a recent one in philosophy, see C. Taylor, *Sources of the Self: The Making of the Modern Identity* (Cambridge, Mass., 1989); in psychology, L. Sass, *Madness and Modernism: Insanity in the Light of Art, Literature, and Thought* (New York, 1992); in anthropology, M. Manganaro, ed., *Modernist Anthropology: From Fieldwork to Text* (Princeton, 1990).

137–138. "certainly in Indonesia and Morocco": Sukarno, *Surat-surat dari Endeh,* in K. Goenadi and H. M. Nasution, eds., *Di Bendera Revolusi* (Jakarta, 1959), p. 340 (for Indonesia buffs, the word was *keuptodatean*). W. D. Swearingen, *Moroccan Mirages: Agrarian Dreams and Deceptions, 1912–1986* (Princeton, 1987), p. 151. The "modernization" formula did not, of course, appear whole and full-blown only after independence in either country, but was a leading theme in the liberal apologetics of late colonialism. For the Indonesian case, see J. S. Furnivall, *Netherlands India* (Cambridge, 1944), esp. chs. 7–13; for the Moroccan, A. Ayache, *Le Maroc* (Paris, 1956), esp. parts 2–4.

141. "A book": D. Wilhelm, *Emerging Indonesia* (London, 1980). J. Hureau, *Le Maroc aujourd'hui,* 3rd ed. (Paris, 1974).

141. "Hassan II's memoirs": King Hassan II of Morocco, *The Challenge* (London, 1978); orig. pub. as *Le Défi* (Paris, 1977). The epigraphs are, from the Quran, "He who attaches himself closely to God will be directed onto the straight path. Attach yourselves together closely in a pact with God; do not divide yourselves"; from Machiavelli *(On Livy),* "If to conspire against a Prince is a dubious, dangerous and foolhardy venture, to conspire against two Princes is futile and insane."

141. "in the opening chapter": Soeharto, *Soeharto: My Thoughts, Words, and Deeds* (Jakarta, 1989), p. 4, orig. pub. as *Soeharto: Pikiran, Ucapan, dan Tindakan Saya* (Jakarta, 1989); cited (though with an incorrect page number) in M. R. J. Vatikiotis, *Indonesian Politics under Suharto: Order, Development and Pressure for Change* (London, 1993), p. 9.

142. "essentialism" and "epochalism": See C. Geertz, "After the Revolution: The Fate of Nationalism in the New States," in *The Interpretation of Cultures* (New York, 1973), pp. 234–254, esp. 240–241. I have discussed some of the effects of this tension in connection with the Indonesian Festival of the Arts, held in the United States in 1990–91, in "The Year of Living Culturally," *New Republic,* October 21, 1991.

142. "the difference is not great": Indonesia's estimated per capita income was a bit above $600 on a $94 million GDP in 1989; Morocco's, a bit below $1000 on a $22 million one. Morocco's 1985–89 real GDP growth was around five percent, as was Indonesia's. World Bank, *Trends in Developing Economies* (Washington D.C., 1991), pp. 278–284, 372–377. More recently, Indonesia's growth has accelerated somewhat, but per capita income is still only about $600, about the same as in Egypt. "Wealth in Its Grasp: A Survey of Indonesia," *The Economist,* April 17, 1993, p. 3. Indonesia is the fourth-largest country in the world in population terms, having moved up from fifth with the dissolution of the USSR; Morocco is (about) the thirty-fifth. *World Development Report, 1992* (New York, 1992), table 1.

143. "examples of them, concrete and actual": Some of the material to follow has already appeared, in a different form, in C. Geertz, "'Popular Art' and the Javanese Tradition," *Indonesia,* October 1990, pp. 77–94; and "*Toutes Directions:* Reading the Signs in an Urban Sprawl," *International Journal of Middle Eastern Studies* 21 (1989): 321–335.

143. "A 'madrasah,'": On types of religious schools in Indonesia, see C. Geertz, *The Religion of Java* (Glencoe, Ill., 1960), part 2, and "Modernization in a Muslim Society: The Indonesian Case," in R. N. Bellah, ed., *Religion and Progress in Modern Asia* (New York, 1966), pp. 93–108. See also M. Junus, *Sedjarah Pendidikan Islam di Indonesia* (Jakarta, 1960), and K. D. Steenbrink, "Pesantren, Madrasah, Sekolah, recent ontwikkelingen in indonische islamonderricht" (thesis, Catholic University of Nijmigen, the Netherlands, 1974). In recent years, reforms in the pesantren system have brought some pesantrens closer to the madrasah pattern (see *Direktori Pesantren, I,* P3M, Jakarta, 1985), and there has been some introduction of rather elementary (and rather officialized) religious teaching in the state schools.

144. "modernist-reformist, 'scripturalist' leanings": On "scripturalism" as a denomination for reformist Islam, see C. Geertz, *Islam Observed: Religious Development in Morocco and Indonesia* (New Haven, 1968), ch. 3. With the reinvigoration of political Islam, the question of what to call the various sorts of religio-ideological movements which have appeared—"fundamentalism," "integralism," "traditionalism," "extremism," "radicalism," "Salafism," "Khomeinism," "literalism," "Islamism," etc., has grown somewhat heated. No general term will really suit, given the diversity of orientations, but it still seems to me that "scripturalism" is both more descriptive of the general

direction of things and less loaded than most. For an interesting discussion of this problem that plumps, reasonably enough, for "Islamism," see F. Burgat and W. Dowell, *The Islamic Movement in North Africa* (Austin, 1993), pp. 8–41.

151–152. "the look of the built environment": On Moroccan architecture and city layout in general, and especially on the impact of French planning upon it, see G. Wright, *The Politics of Design in French Colonial Urbanism* (Chicago, 1991), ch. 3; P. Rabinow, *French Modern: Norms and Forms of the Social Environment* (Cambridge, Mass., 1989), ch. 9.

152. "that French word that translates": On the notion of *citadinité* see M. Naciri, "Regards sur l'évolution de la citadinité au Maroc," in *Symposium franco-britannique sur La ville arabo-musulmane* (London, 1984), pp. 37–59, to whose work I am much indebted. See also M. Naciri, "Les politiques urbaines: Instruments de pouvoir ou outils de développement?" in J. Métral and G. Mutin, eds., *Etudes sur le monde arabe,* no. 1, Lyon, pp. 13–42; M. Naciri, "Politique urbaine et 'politiques' de l'habitat au Maroc: Incertitudes d'une stratégie," ibid., pp. 71–98; M. Naciri and M. Ameur, "L'urbanisation clandestine au Maroc: Un champ d'action pour les classes moyennes," *Revue Tiers Monde* 26 (1985): 80–92.

153. "discussion in scholarly circles": For varying views, from varying disciplines, see J. L. Abu-Lughod, "The Islamic City—Historic Myth, Islamic Essence, and Contemporary Relevance," *International Journal of Middle East Studies* 19 (1987): 155–176; J. Bisson and J.-F. Troin, eds., *Présent et avenir des médinas (de Marrakech à Alep)* (Tours, 1982); A. Bouhdiba and D. Chevallier, eds., *La ville arabe dans l'Islam* (Paris, 1982); K. Brown, "The Uses of a Concept: 'The Muslim City,'" in P. Solé et al., *Middle Eastern Cities in Comparative Perspective* (London, 1986), pp. 60–68; D. Eickelman, "Is There an Islamic City? The Making of a Quarter in a Moroccan Town," *International Journal of Middle East Studies* 5 (1974): 274–294; B. S. Hakim, *Arabic-Islamic Cities* (London, 1986); R. Holod, ed., *Toward an Architecture in the Spirit of Islam* (Philadelphia, 1978); A. Hourani and S. M. Stern, eds., *The Islamic City* (Philadelphia, 1970); A. Y. Saqqaf, ed., *The Middle East City: Ancient Traditions Confront a Modern World* (New York, 1987); R. B. Serjeant, ed., *The Islamic City* (Paris, 1980); L. C. Brown, ed., *From Madina to Metropolis* (Princeton, 1973); I. Lapidus, ed., *Middle Eastern Cities, Ancient, Islamic, and Contemporary Middle Eastern Urbanism: A Symposium* (Berkeley, 1969), esp. part 2. For an historical treatment: I. Lapidus, *Muslim Cities in the Later Middle Ages* (Cambridge, Mass., 1967).

153. "the despised 'orientalism'": For the critique of orientalism, see E. Said, *Orientalism* (New York, 1978).

154. "Old Medinas," "New Medinas": On the structural composition of Moroccan cities, see, inter alia, M. Naciri, "Salé: Étude de géographie ur-

baine," *Revue de Géographie du Maroc* 3–4 (1963): 13–82; J. Abu-Lughod, *Rabat: Urban Apartheid in Morocco* (Princeton, 1980); K. Brown, *The People of Salé: Tradition and Change in a Moroccan City, 1820–1930* (Cambridge, Mass., 1976); D. Eickelman, *Moroccan Islam: Tradition and Society in a Pilgrimage Center* (Austin, 1976); J. Berque, "Médinas, villesneuves et bidonvilles," *Le Cahiers de Tunisie,* 21–22, pp. 5–42; R. LeTourneau, *Fès avant le protectorat: Étude économique et sociale d'une ville de l'occident musulman* (Casablanca, 1949). For Sefrou, L. Rosen, "Social Identity and Points of Attachment: Approaches to Social Organization," in C. Geertz, H. Geertz, and L. Rosen, *Meaning and Order in Moroccan Society: Three Essays in Cultural Analysis* (Cambridge, 1979), pp. 19–122; H. Chafai, "Naissance et développement d'une municipalité marocaine sous le Protectorat Français: Sefrou, 1912–1956" (thesis, University of Paris-I, 1985). M. Yakhlef, "Taṭawwur adāwat al-siyāsat al-maḥalliyya bi madīna Ṣufrū, awākhir al-qarn 19–1956" (thesis, Faculty of Letters, University Mohammed al-Khamis, Rabat, 1986). The author of this last study, Mhd. Yakhlef, was the leader of the Socialist party in Sefrou and head of the city's municipal council during the period 1976–1983. Born in an Arabic-speaking rural area about a dozen kilometers from the town, he moved to the town sometime in the early seventies to become a schoolteacher. I did not know him during my earlier stays in Sefrou. (He wrote to me in Princeton for a copy of my and my colleagues' book on the town, *Meaning and Order,* while he was head of the council, and had his French wife, an English teacher in the Sefrou schools, translate it for him.) But he was of enormous help during my investigation of the whole affair described here, not only in himself, but, extremely well respected, even by those who had wished him harm when he was in power, by introducing me to knowledgeable people on both sides of the political divide. After the Socialist defeat he moved to Fez, both for safety's sake and to pursue his advanced degree in history at Mhd. V University in Rabat while teaching at the state university in Fez. He is, of course, in no way responsible for my descriptions and interpretations, some of which he would surely contest; but—as in the case of Mhd. Yazid in Pare, who would also doubtless contest some of my conclusions—I learned a very great deal from him about how a society looks to someone for whom it is not (or not only) an object of inquiry but one of hope and uncertainty.

154. "reading-in": R. Wollheim, *Painting as Art* (Princeton, 1987). Wollheim's term is, of course, a reworking for the visual arts of Wittgenstein's "seeing as" conception of sense-making in general. L. Wittgenstein, *Philosophical Investigations* (New York, 1953), pp. 193ff.

154. "ornament, design, and the particularity of spaces": For a searching examination of the role of ornament in Islam and Islamic art (and in art more generally), see O. Grabar, *The Mediation of Ornament* (Princeton, 1992).

156. "the traditional bazaars": For a description of the old city bazaars in Sefrou, see C. Geertz, "Suq: The Bazaar Economy in Sefrou," in C. Geertz, H. Geertz, and L. Rosen, *Meaning and Order,* pp. 123–313.

156. "reasserting its own ascendancy, reasserted theirs": On the "effacement and survival of the notables" in the immediate Independence and post-Independence periods in Morocco generally, see R. Leveau, *Le fellah marocain, défenseur du trône* (Paris, 1976), esp. part 1. For the Sefrou elite during the colonial period, see Yakhlef, "Taṭawwur adwāt al-siyāsat al-maḥalliyya bi madīna Ṣufrū, awākhir al-qarn 19–1956"; Chafai, "Naissance et développement d'une municipalité marocaine sous le Protectorat Français."

159. "as the royalist newspaper": "Pour un salon du bâtiment de l'urbanisme et de l'architecture," *Le Matin du Sahara,* March 1, 1986 (my translation). This is not a transcript of the king's speech, which I was unable to obtain, but a reporter's (more or less official, considering the source) commentary on it in connection with an architectural exhibition in Casablanca that followed upon it. My own summary is thus a paraphrase of a paraphrase, filled out with accounts from Sefroui informants who heard, as I did not, the original speech.

160. "in a word": Ibid. The tendency for political leaders in the Muslim world to see architecture and city planning as critical to the sustenance of an authentic Islamic consciousness in the modern world, and as threatened by "sudden affluence," "an unprecedented growth of building activity," "urbanization without urbanism," and "ruralization of city life," is very general: see, for example, His Highness the Aga Khan, "Opening Remarks," in Holod, *Toward an Architecture,* pp. viii–ix, and Hassan Bin Talal, Crown Prince of Jordan, "Introduction," in Saqqaf, *The Middle East City,* pp. ix–xiii, from which these quotes are taken. As for Hassan himself, his critique of Sefrou as vulgar and ostentatious has perhaps a bit of a hollow ring, as the following, entitled "A Passion for Palaces," from *The Economist,* April 14, 1990, p. 52, suggests:

> King Hassan's new palace at Agadir was inaugurated on March 3rd. It is decorated with carved cedarwood, gold leaf, marble and mosaic. One room contains an 11-ton Venetian crystal chandelier. Within the palace grounds lie three golf courses (one has only nine holes): the king is an enthusiastic golfer. The royal pile reputedly cost $360m. It is his tenth palace.
>
> "The government," said the king in his first speech from the Agadir palace, "must reduce all expenditure." He warned fellow Moroccans of hard times ahead. The country has widening trade and budget deficits. Besides, it needs to pay for the king's 11th palace, in the Saharan oasis of Tafilalt, the ancestral home of his Alawite dynasty. His 12th palace is planned for Nador on the Mediterranean coast. Agadir apart, he has

palaces in Rabat (three), Meknes, Fez, Marrakesh, Casablanca, Tangiers and Ifrane.

Why so many? Officials say the king rules Morocco "from the saddle." King Hassan, a monarch of a type extinct in Europe, wants to be seen, ruling, in every part of his kingdom. The royal entourage is several hundred strong. Palaces are needed to accommodate them all.

Few Moroccans seem to mind. Many say they are happy to indulge a man who is not just a king but also "Commander of the Faithful." Only the Islamic fundamentalists have objected outright. Some years ago, Sheikh Abdesalam Yassine, leader of the outlawed Al Adl wa Hihsane ("Justice and Welfare") party, attacked the king's extravagance in a 104-page open letter. Sheikh Yassine is under house arrest in the town of Salé. In January his party was dissolved. Last month 21 of his supporters were jailed.

In Casablanca the huge Hassan II mosque is nearing completion, at a cost of over $400m. Its marbled nave has room for 20,000 worshippers. "They say it is the biggest mosque in the world," Sheikh Yassine said recently. "That is good. We hope one day to be allowed to pray there."

The popular joke in Sefrou about the mosque was of two worshipers who go to it but can't get in for the crowd. One says they should complain; the other says, "Don't do that! He will only build another one!"

162. "medina houses are turned radically inward": For an insightful discussion of the classical medina house (*dar*), see Hakim, *Arabic-Islamic Cities,* pp. 95–96. Hakim, who is concerned mostly with Tunisia, outlines three "Islamic and ethical requirements" for such houses: privacy, interdependence, and *bāṭin* vs. *ẓāhir.* Of the last, he remarks: "One of the essential values in Islam is emphasis on the Batin of the Zahir (the external aspect of the self or a thing). For example, internal goodness and well-being are emphasized and arrogance discouraged. The courtyard house and its aggregate organizational pattern is suitable for the application of this principle. Hence we find that the external walls are kept simple and relatively bare with few openings. The courtyard as the central important space is decorated— when the owner can afford it—to a high level of artistic sophistication, despite the fact that it is accessible to and enjoyed by only the occupants, and occasionally their relatives and close friends." There are, of course, other reasons, traditionally, for this pattern: the desire, in the absence of an effective security system, to conceal wealth from predatory view, and a general emphasis on civic and religious equality.

163. "the urban veil": Rural women in Morocco are largely unveiled; city women, at least in so traditional a place as Sefrou, are, after marriage, mostly veiled as a sign of both their religious propriety and their urbanity. It is

tempting to place the house facades within this larger, very subtle system of symbolic "faciality," but the issue is complex. On "the veil" in Morocco more generally, see F. Mernissi, *Beyond the Veil: Male-Female Dynamics in a Modern Muslim Society,* rev. ed. (Bloomington, Ind., 1987).

164–165. "an Arabic-language newspaper": "Discrimination among the Inhabitants of the Quarter Bni Saffar in Getting Drinkable Water," *Al-'Alam,* February 15, 1988. *Al-'Alam* is the paper of the scripturalist Islamic party, Istiqlal, which, since the Socialists were broken in Sefrou, has emerged again as the main local oppositional voice. I am grateful to Dr. Abderrahmane El Moudden for bringing this letter to my attention and for help in translating the highly flowery prose in which it is cast.

165. "Auden's famous line": "Petition," in *The Collected Poetry of W. H. Auden* (New York, 1945).

167. "an Indian story": J. Bruner, *Acts of Meaning* (Cambridge, Mass., 1990), p. 150.

Index